THE COMPLETE PESCATARIAN

COOKBOOK

99+ RECIPES TO START YOUR HEALTHY LIFESTYLE ON

A BUDGET + 3 DAYS MEAL PLAN

Andrew Ball

INTRODUCTION

Americans have started putting a lot of thought into the foods they consume in the last decade. Not only are people concerned with ensuring they consume nutritious foods to give their bodies plenty of nutrients, but they are also involved in ensuring they eat foods that are not full of preservatives or additives. People are searching for ways to consume less processed foods that are more sustainable for the whole world. These trends have recently led many Americans to become vegetarians or even vegans, all of which are good options. However, some people have discovered that when they exclude all animal protein from their diets, they do not get enough protein in their diets and live healthily through a well-balanced pescatarian diet.

Instead of losing all animal protein, more people are transitioning to diets like fish. That's because fish produce a lot of nutritious protein, are low in fat, have healthy fats, and are renewable resources. In Alaska, for example, fishers help conserve the shellfish population by harvesting only prime males that meet minimum size requirements. Fishers may thus be sure that they do not harvest fish that are still growing and do not harvest the female fish to keep the shellfish population safe through reproduction. Consumers will consume the prime males without having to worry about destroying the fish population in Alaska.

Recent books like The Omnivore's Dilemma and movies like Food Inc. have increased American awareness of food industry activities and the foods Americans consume. Unfortunately, the fishing industry has gained much less publicity than the meat industry. They can eat a healthy amount of fish without damaging the ecosystem.

Americans should enjoy a balanced pescatarian diet instead of going all the way to the extreme of being vegetarian or vegan to get the nutritious value they need without affecting the environment in the same way as a diet full of beef, pork, or chicken does.

TABLE OF CONTENT

Chapter 1. Pescatarian Breakfast Recipes

1. Pumpkin Oatmeal

Ingredients

- Two Cups of 1-Minute Oats

- 1 1/4 cup of milk with almonds

- 1 1/4 cup of milk with almonds

- 3/4 cup of canned pumpkin

- Light-brown sugar 1 tablespoon

- 2 Teaspoon Pumpkin Spice

- Pinch of salt

- Chips with 1/4 cup butterscotch

- 1/4 cup of optional white chocolate chips

- 1/4 cup of optional chopped walnuts

- Cool Whip Topping

Directions

1. Whisk all ingredients together in a microwave-safe bowl except for the optional toppings, walnuts, and whipped toppings.

2. Microwave on high for around two minutes, or until the consistency is needed (for thinner oatmeal, add more milk. For thicker, less milk)

3. Let it take about one minute to rest and serve hot. For an extra tasty treat, top with walnuts, extra butterscotch, and white chocolate chips, and a refreshing whip!

2. Pumpkin Muffins

Ingredients

- 2 Cups of all-in-one flour
- 1/2 cup of brown sugar
- 1 Tablespoon powder for baking
- 1 big egg
- 1 glass of milk
- 1 Vanilla Extract Teaspoon
- 4 Seasoned butter, melted
- 1/2 Cup of canned pumpkin (not packed with pumpkin pie)
- 1/2 Cup of roasted pumpkin seeds
- 1 Seasoning Teaspoon Pumpkin Pie
- The salt squeeze
- Cinnamon pinch

Directions

1. In a small bowl, blend the milk, egg, vanilla, and pumpkin puree until the mixture is smooth.

2. 2) Mix the dry ingredients like the pumpkin seeds together in a separate, larger cup.

3. 3) Into the dry ingredients, incorporate the wet ingredients, and stir to blend. Stir in the butter, then melted.

4. 4) Butter 12 muffin tins and break between the tins with muffin batter.

5. 5) Bake the muffins for 18-20 minutes at 375 degrees until they are lightly browned and baked.

6. 6) Shortly allow cooling before serving. Serve if you can with pumpkin butter!

3. Oatmeal Cookies with Brown Butter Icing

Ingredients

- 2 Cups of old styled rolled oats

- 1 All-purpose cup of flour

- 1/2 tbsp baking soda

- 1/2 Cinnamon Teaspoon

- 1/4 Cardamom Teaspoon

- Freshly grated nutmeg 1/4 teaspoon

- 1/4 of a teaspoon of salt

- 1 1/2 sticks, 12 tablespoons of melted and cooled unsalted butter

- 1 1/2 cups of brown sugar loosely packed

- 1 egg + 1 yolk of one egg, at room temperature

- 2 teaspoons extract of vanilla

Icing Brown Butter

- 1/4 cup unsalted butter

- 1/2 to 3/4 cup sugar powder

- 1/2 tsp extract of vanilla

- 1 1/2 cups of milk

Directions

1. Preheat the oven to 350 degrees F. Line a sheet (or 2) of parchment paper to bake.

2. Place half the oats in a food processor and pulse until the oats, some flour-like, are chopped up, but some pieces remain. Mix all the oats, flour, baking soda, cinnamon, cardamom, nutmeg, and salt together in a dish. Whisk along.

3. Whisk the melted butter and the brown sugar together in a large bowl until smooth. Whisk in the yolk of the egg and egg, then the vanilla, until smooth and mixed. Stir in the dry ingredients, mixing until a dough forms. Take a large spoon.

4. Use an ice cream scoop to scoop the dough out (you want about 2 tablespoons of dough) and put it 2 inches apart on the parchment paper. On a baking sheet, I put 6 because they're going to spread! Bake for 12 to 14 minutes or until thin and chewy, golden on the edges. Remove and leave to cool.

4. Strawberry Chia Overnight Oats

Ingredients

Oats

- 1/3 cup of rolling oats

- 1/2 cup Silk Nutmilk

- 1 Chia seeds 1 Tbsp

- 1 tsp honey (or maple syrup)

- of Vanilla

- 1 Tbsp seed jam of strawberry chia (see recipe below)

Jam (you're not going to need it all):

- 1 cup of chopped strawberries

- 1 Tbsp (or maple syrup) honey

- 1 Chia seeds 1 Tbsp

Optional Overhangs:

- Strawberry jam with chia seed

- Strawberries sliced

Directions

1. To make Granola combine the oats, almond milk, chia seeds, honey (or maple syrup if vegan), vanilla, and jam in a jar or bowl and blend well.

2. Tightly cover with a cap or plastic wrap and chill overnight.

3. In a small saucepan over medium heat, add chopped strawberries to make the jam and occasionally stir until they become syrupy around 5 minutes.

4. Using a potato masher or the back of your spoon to mash the strawberries and extract them from the sun. Add honey (or maple syrup) and chia seeds, blend well and leave to thicken for around 5 minutes.

5. With a dollop of jelly, sliced strawberries, and granola, top overnight oats. Experience!

5. Dutch Baby Pancake

Ingredients

- 2 Cups of 1 "pieces of fresh asparagus cut

- 1/2 California cup Milk

- 1/2 cup gluten-free all-purpose flour OR standard all-purpose flour

- 4 Grand Eggs

- 1/8 teaspoon of salt

- 2 teaspoons butter from California

- Fresh black ground pepper to taste

- 1 cup California Monterey Jack cheese shredded

- 2 cups Microgreens

Directions

1. Preheat the oven to 450 ° F.

2. Steam the asparagus onto the stovetop OR in the microwave in a medium-sized steamer pan up to tender-crisp.

3. Combine the flour, milk, eggs, and salt in a mixer while the asparagus is steaming, and blend until smooth.

4. In a large cast-iron pan or ovenproof dish over medium heat, melt the butter. Add the steamed asparagus to taste, plus fresh ground black pepper, then saute for 1 minute.

5. In the pan, pour the batter over the asparagus, top with the shredded cheese, and move the skillet to the oven to bake for 15 minutes or until the pancake is golden brown and puffed.

6. Top with microgreens, cut into wedges and serve while still warm.

6. Pumpkin Cinnamon Rolls

Ingredients

Dough

- 1 1/2 of a c. Entire Milk

- 1⁄2 C. Oil from Vegetables

- 1/2 of a c. Zucker

- Active Dry Yeast 1 box (2 1/4 teaspoons)

- 1 of a c. Kitten Puree

- 4 C. C. All-purpose Meal

- 1/2 hp. Ground cane

- 1/4. Tsp. Nutmeg Field

- 1/4. Tsp Ginger Land

- 1/2 of a c. (supplementary) All-purpose Flour

- 1/2 hp. Baked Soda

- 1/2 hp. (Heaping) Powder for Baking

- 1/2 hp. Salt The Salt

Filling

- 1 1/2 cup butter stick, melted

- 1/2 of a c. sugar

- 1/2 of a c. Sugar

- 1/2 tsp. cinnamon

- Tsp. 1/4. Nutmeg Field

- 1/2 tsp. Ginger Land

- 1 of a c. Finely cut pecans

Frosting

- 8 oz. Cheese Cream, Softened

- 1/2 lb. Powdered sugar

- 1/4 of a c. whole milk

- 2 tbsp. Butter to stir

- Dash of Salt

- For Rolling, Extra Flour

- Extra milk, to thin

- For The Baking Pans, Extra Butter

Directions

Dough

1. Combine 1 1/2 cups of whole milk, 1/2 of vegetable oil, and 1/2 of sugar in a large saucepan.

2. Remove the pan from the stove and allow it to cool until the mixture is warm to the touch but not too hot. Sprinkle the leaves over the liquid surface and allow to sit for 5 minutes.

3. Stir the pumpkin puree together until mixed.

4. Combine with 1/2 teaspoon cinnamon, 1/4 teaspoon nutmeg, and 1/4 teaspoon ginger for 4 cups of flour.

5. Sprinkle it and stir it in the saucepan until it all comes together.

6. Cover the casserole with a dish towel, and set for 1 hour in a warm, draft-free location.

7. The mixture should be very puffy after 1 hour and at least double in size. Add 1/2 cup of flour, baking soda, baking powder, and salt until fully mixed together.

Rolls

1. Preheat the oven to 375 degrees. Drizzle butter into 3 pie pans (or a larger baking platter) and spread all over the bottom of the pans.

2. Turn the dough out onto a floured surface, then press it into a rectangular shape. Sprinkle generously with flour if it is overly sticky and treat it / flour until it is easier to handle.

3. Flour a rolling pin and roll the dough up about 10 inches by 30 inches into a long rectangle.

4. Drizzle the melted butter 1 stick over the dough and smear it with your fingers all over the surface. Mix the 1/2 cup sugar, 1/2 cup brown sugar, cinnamon, nutmeg, and ginger together.

5. Sprinkle all of this over the dough board, covering all of the melted butter. Sprinkle the chopped pecans with 1/2 cup to 3/4 cup.

6. Using a "typewriter" motion beginning at the top to roll the dough toward you into a large log. Roll it up tightly as you go so be smooth and tidy with the rolls.

7. Pinch the seam closed when it is all rolled, and switch the rollover so that the seam is facing down.

8. In the buttered pans, slice 1/2 to 3/4 inch slices and put them.

9. Enable them to rise for 20 minutes, then bake around the edges for 15-18 minutes or until good, golden brown.

Frosting

1. While the rolls bake, frosting is achieved by mixing all the frosting ingredients in an electric mixer's cup.
2. If you'd like a thinner icing, beat until soft, adding more milk. If used, add maple flavoring and beat until blended.
3. The second they come out of the oven, slice the rolls. Sprinkle over the frosting with additional walnuts, then let them rest before serving for 15 minutes.
4. Tasty! Delicious!

7. Shrimp and Scallion Pancake

Ingredients

- 2 cloves of garlic, minced

- 3/4 of the salt teaspoon

- 3/4 of a water cup

- 2 beaten eggs

- 1 tbs sesame oil

- 3/4 cup flour, all-purpose

- 1 bunch of scallions, thinly sliced only green pieces, white parts gone

- 1/2 red peppered bell, stemmed, seeded, and finely sliced

- 1/2 pound, medium shrimp, peeled and halved lengthwise

- 1/4 canola oil

Directions

1. In a wide bowl, whisk in the garlic, salt, water, eggs, and sesame oil. Attach the flour, and whisk until a smooth batter forms. The scallions, bell pepper, and shrimp fold in.

2. Into a large non-stick skillet set over medium-high heat, pour half of the canola oil. Pour half the batter in when it's wet.

3. Using a spatula for further spreading the batter around the skillet. Cook per side for 2 minutes, or until well browned.

4. Drain the pancake with the rest of the oil and batter on some paper towel, and repeat the process.

8. Banana Almond Mocha Smoothie

Ingredients

- 1 cup spinach kale for baby, or other greens

- 1 cup of unsweetened almond milk or cashew milk

- 1/2 cup cottage cheese with or plain Greek yogurt

- 1 tablespoon of chia seeds

- 1 Instant Teaspoon Coffee

- 1 table litre of cocoa powder

- 1 teaspoon of butter with almonds

- 1 Frozen banana which is cut into pieces

- For a thicker smoothie, add 4 more ice cubes to

- 1 tsp. of honey sugar, stevia, or the appropriate sweetener to taste, if necessary

Directions

1. Place the ingredients in the order indicated in your Blendtec or any other blender.

2. Use the Smoothie loop or pulse a few times, then increase steadily to full velocity, stopping until the desired texture is reached.

9. Fruit & Nuts Oatmeal Breakfast

Ingredients

Dry Materials

- 3/4 cup oats rolled

- 1/2 cup, chopped pecans

- 1/2 cup of finely shredded undulating coconut

- 1/2 of a dried cup of cranberries

- 1/4 cup whole wheat flour

- 2 tbsp. Chia seeds

- 1/2 tsp. Salt, I use salt from the Himalayas

- 1/2 tsp. Cinnamon Ground

- 1/4 tsp. powder for baking

- 1/4 Tsp. Baking soda

Wet Materials

- 2 big eggs at room temperature

- 2 tbsp. coconut oil melted

- 1/2 cup fluffy butter for peanuts

- 1/4 cup honey unpasteurized

- 1/2 tsp. Vanilla pure extract

- 16-20 halves of pecan, for decorating

Directions

1. Preheat the oven to 350 ° F. Grease a 9 "baking pan with parchment paper and line it; set aside.

2. Combine the dry ingredients in a large bowl and mix with a whisk or fork until mixed very well.

3. Combine the wet ingredients in a smaller bowl and whisk until smooth and combine very well; pour over the dry ingredients and mix well with a rubber spatula.

4. Move the dough to the prepared pan and spread as evenly as possible, if desired, then press the pecan halves gently over the surface.

5. Bake for 23-25 minutes or until the top is pleasant brown and a toothpick inserted into the cake's middle comes out clean.

6. Place the pan on a cooling rack and cool the bars for at least 1 hour, then take it out of the pan and break it into 16 to 20 bars.

7. For up to a week, hold the bars in an airtight container in a cool, dry spot.

10. Banana Bread with Brown Butter Glaze

Ingredients

Bread

- 3 tbsp. Unsalted butter

- 3/4 of a cup of dark brown sugar

- 3 bananas, medium ripe, sliced

- 2 Cups of all-purpose flour

- 3/4 teaspoon of soda for baking

- 1/2 tsp. of salt

- 1/2. Cup buttermilk

- Canola oil for 3 tablespoons

- 2 tbsp. of rum

- 2 large eggs

Glaze

- Unsalted butter for 1 tablespoon

- 1/3 cup of sugar for confectioners

- 2 Half and a half teaspoons

Directions

Bread

1. Preheat oven to 350 ° C. Grease a loaf pan of 9 x 5 ".

2. In a skillet, put butter. Melt over high-medium sun. Add the brown sugar and bananas and cook, stirring occasionally, for 4 minutes.

3. Withdraw from the sun. Cool down for 10 minutes.

4. Move the mixture of cooled bananas to a large tub. Use a medium-speed electric mixer, beat until smooth.

5. Whisk the rice, baking soda, and salt together. Placed on aside.

6. In a big bowl, mix your buttermilk, canola oil, rum, and eggs.

7. Apply the flour mixture, alternating with the buttermilk mixture, to the banana mixture in 3 or 4 portions. Simply blend until combined.

8. Move batter to the ready-made pan. Bake for 1 hour, or until moist crumbs come out with a pick inserted into the middle.

9. Cold bread for 10 minutes in a saucepan on a wire rack. Then, to cool completely, remove the bread from the pan to a wire rack.

Glaze

1. Put the butter in a small casserole dish. Cook until it starts browning, over medium-high heat.

2. Withdraw the butter from the sun. Apply sugar and half-and-a-half of the confectioners. Until smooth, whisk.

3. Glaze Drizzle over toast. Enable until the glaze sets to stand.

11. Cinnamon Raisin French Toast

Ingredients

- 4-6 slices of cinnamon raisin bread (may replace gluten-free).

- 3 eggs

- 1/4 cup milk (dairy-free substitutions can be used)

- 1 tsp. vanilla

- 1 teaspoon of cinnamon

- 1/3 cup sugar

- 1 cup of bread crumbs (you can use them without gluten)

- 1 stick (1/2 cup) coconut oil or butter

- Maple syrup used to serve

Directions

1. In a cup, whisk together eggs, milk, vanilla, half the cinnamon, and half the sugar until smooth. Place the bowl aside.

2. Stir together the breadcrumbs, remaining sugar, and cinnamon in a pie pan or shallow dish. Apply two tablespoons of melted butter or coconut oil and whisk with a fork until the breadcrumbs are moistened slightly.

3. Heat the remaining butter or coconut oil in a non-stick skillet over medium-low heat

4. Dip each slice of bread into the egg mixture, turning the bread to coat both sides. Place the breadcrumbs with each slice of bread and cover. To cover completely, press the breadcrumbs onto the slices.

5. Place the bread in the skillet and allow the toast to cook on one side for 4-6 minutes, then flip over and cook on the other side for another 2-3 minutes until the breadcrumbs have browned.

6. When cooked, remove the bread pieces from the pan, then put them on the plate and serve with maple syrup.

12. Black Bottom Oatmeal Pie

Ingredients

Crust

- 1 1/4 cups all-purpose flour

- 1 tbsp. of granulated sugar

- 1/2 tablespoon of salt

- 1/2 cup cold unsalted butter, cut into 1/2-inch cubes

- 2 to 4 spoonfuls of cold water

Filling

- 1 & 1/2 cups of oats, rolled

- 1/4 cup cream, strong

- 4 ounces of bittersweet, finely minced chocolate

- 3/4 of a cup of light brown sugar, packed

- 5 Tablespoon of unsalted butter,

- 1/2 tablespoon of salt

- 1/4 teaspoon ginger field

- 1 Cup of dark maize syrup

- 2 teaspoons of vinegar from cider

- 1 Vanilla Teaspoon Extract

- 4 Grand Eggs

Directions

Crust

1. In a wide bowl, whisk together the flour, sugar, and salt. Use a pastry mixer or fork to add the butter and mix until the mixture resembles coarse flour and forms small pea-sized chunks. Add 1 spoonful of water, and proceed to blend. Add more water as needed, until a dough forms, 1 tablespoon at a time.

2. Tightly seal the dough in plastic wrap. Cool for at least 2 hours.

3. Remove dough from the fridge. If required, let it rest for 10 to 15 minutes at room temperature until slightly softened but still cold.

4. Preheat the oven to 325 degrees.

5. Slight surface for flour work. Roll out dough into a circle about 1/8-inch thick.

6. Move the dough to a 9-inch pie plate which is lightly greased. From the sides, trim any excess dough.

7. Push the knuckle of one finger into the rim of the crust for an easy fluted tip, while keeping two fingers on either side of your knuckle about half-inch apart. Repeat around the crust's entire edge.

8. Line the crust with parchment paper so that either side of the paper overhangs. Place pie weights (or dried beans) in the pan.

9. Bake for about 20 minutes. Remove the lining and weights, then brush with an egg wash. * Bake for an additional 3 minutes.

10. Serve absolutely cool.

Filling

1. Increase the oven's temperature to 350 °.

2. Using a rimmed baking sheet lined with parchment paper to spread the oats. Bake 10 to 12 minutes until toasted, stirring occasionally. Set to cool aside.

3. Put heavy cream into a heavy casserole. Bring it over medium heat to a boil.

4. Remove from heat and mix in the chocolate. Let sit for 5 minutes.

5. Gently whisk until you get a smooth ganache. Move to pie shell, and uniformly distributed.

6. Place the pie in the freezer while the rest of the filling is finished.

7. Reduce the temperature of the oven to 325 °.

8. In a wide bowl, put the brown sugar, butter, salt, and ginger together. Whisk to merge.

9. Stir in corn, vinegar, and vanilla. Whisk once fused. Add eggs, then combine well after each addition, one at a time. Stir the oats in.

10. Remove the pie crust from the freezer and put on a baking sheet with rims. Pour in the crust with the filling.

11. Bake for 55 to 60 minutes or until the edges are set and gently puffed, and the centre is nearly set.

12. On a wire rack, cool absolutely.

13. Serve at room temperature or hotter.

13. Morning Meal Sausage Gravy

Ingredients

- 1 lb. sausage

- 2 cups 2 percent milk (complete is great also)
- 1/4 cup entire wheat bread
- salt and a lot of pepper to flavour

Directions

1. Cook sausage from skillet.
2. Add flour and blend cook for about a minute.
3. Insert two cups of milk.
4. Whisk whilst gravy thickens and bubbles.
5. Add pepper and salt and keep to taste until flawless.
6. Let stand a minute or so to ditch and function over several snacks.

14. Pumpkin Spice Porridge

Ingredients

- 2 cups steel-cut oats, overnight soaked

- 2 cups of water (or milk with vanilla almonds)

- 1 1/2 coconut milk

- 1 cup of pumpkin puree (not combine with pumpkin pie)

- 2 tsp. pumpkin pie spice

- 2 tsp. Cinnamon

- 1/4 teaspoon of fine salt at sea

- 2 Molasses with teaspoons (optional)

- 2 tsp. pure maple syrup

- Tops: coconut/almond milk, sliced pecans, buttered almond, grenade, or cranberries

Directions

1. Strain the oats and rinse them, then add the remaining ingredients to a large pot.

2. Bring to a boil then stir to mix.

3. Reduce to a simmer and cook for about 15 minutes, while stirring intermittently, until the oats are soft.

4. Taste test, if needed, to add more spices or maple syrup.

5. Serve warm with the toppings suggested and enjoy!

15. Easy Egg-white Muffins

Ingredients

- 6 tbsp. or two large egg whites

- Turkey bacon or bacon sausage

- Sharp cheddar cheese or gouda

- Green berry

- Discretionary - lettuce, and hot sauce, hummus, flaxseeds, etc.

Directions

1. At a microwavable safe container, then spray entirely to stop the egg from adhering, then pour egg whites into the dish.

2. Lay turkey bacon or bacon sausage paper towel and then cook.

3. Subsequently, toast your muffin, if preferred.

4. Then put the egg dish in the microwave for 30 minutes. Afterward, with a spoon or fork, then immediately flip the egg within the dish and cook for another 30 minutes.

5. Whilst dish remains hot sprinkle some cheese while preparing sausage.

6. The secret is to get a paste of some kind between each coating to put up the sandwich together, i.e., a very small little bit of hummus or even cheese.

16. Apple Cinnamon Protein Breakfast Cookies

Ingredients

- 1 cup of flour for oats (ground rolled oats)

- 1 cup of oats, rolled

- 1/2 cup plant protein powder (vanilla or unflavoured)

- 1 tbsp. Chia seeds

- 1/2 tbsp. of salt

- 1 tsp. of cinnamon

- 2 very ripe bananas, mashed

- 1 grated apple (no need to peel, of any kind)

- 1/4 cup of unsweetened applesauce

- 2 tsp. of maple syrup

- 1 tsp. vanilla extract

- Gluten-free, or supplement with whole wheat flour if necessary

Directions

1. Preheat the oven to 350 ° F.

2. Line the parchment paper or a silicone mat with a cookie sheet.

3. Combine the oatmeal, rolled oats, protein powder, chia seeds, cinnamon, and salt in a large cup. Mix thoroughly.

4. Combine the mashed banana, grated apple, applesauce, maple syrup, and vanilla extract in a separate dish.

5. To dry, add wet ingredients and stir well until mixed.

6. Shape dough into 12 medium-sized balls, put on a cookie sheet, and then flatten to shape discs with a palm.

7. Bake for 22 minutes.

8. Remove from the cookie sheet and leave on a wire rack to cool down.

9. Will hold in an airtight container for several days, or freeze for several months.

17. Sweet Potato Hash

Ingredients

- 1 inch sweet-potato

- 1/2 red pepper, diced

- 3 green onions, peppermint

- 1 tbsp. of butter

- some powdered carrot smoothies

- Pepper - only a small dab to get a bit of warmth

- pepper and salt to flavour

- scatter of cheddar cheese (optional)

Directions

1. Stab a sweet potato and microwave for 5 minutes.

2. Remove from microwave, peel the skin off, and foliage.

3. At a skillet, on medium-high warmth, place peppers and butter and sauté to get a few minutes.

4. Insert potato bits and keep sautéing.

5. Whilst sauté, add sweeteners, leafy vegetables, and green onions.

6. Insert a dab of cheddar and Revel in!

18. Granola Cake

Ingredients

- 2 cups of butter

- 2 Cups of Sugar

- 2 Cinnamon Tsp.

- 11⁄2 tsp. ground ginger

- 1 tsp. paste vanilla

- 1⁄4 teaspoon allspice

- 2 Eggs

- 1⁄4 cup molasses

- 2 tsp. crystallized chopped ginger

- 2 tsp. powder for baking

- 1⁄2 tsp. soda for baking

- 1⁄2 a cup of milk

- 1⁄2 cup (to blend in) granola

- 1⁄8 cup of granola (for the centre)

- 3 cups of flour

Directions

1. Beat sugar and butter together before adding granola, flour, baking soda, and baking powder to all other ingredients except.

2. Until folding granola in, whisk in flour and growing agents.

3. Apply half the batter to your pan, sprinkle the rest of the batter with reserved granola, and bake at 350 for 40 minutes, or until a knife comes out cleanly.

19. Asparagus, Mushroom Artichoke Strata

Ingredients

- Inch little loaf of sourdough bread

- 4 challah rolls

- 8 eggs

- 2 cups of milk

- 1 teaspoon salt

- 1/4 teaspoon black pepper

- 1 cup Fontina cheese, cut into little chunks

- 1/2 cup shredded Parmesan cheese

- 1 tbsp. butter (I used jojoba)

- 1 teaspoon dried mustard

- 1/2 can of artichoke hearts, sliced

- 1 bunch green onions, grated

- 1 bunch asparagus, cut into 1-inch bits

- 1 10oz package of baby Bella (cremini) mushrooms, chopped

Directions

1. 1. Clean mushrooms and slice, trim asparagus, and cut into 1-inch pieces. Reserve in a bowl and scatter 1/2 teaspoon salt mixture.

2. Drain and dice 1/2 may or modest artichoke hearts.

3. Melt butter in a pan over moderate heat, also sauté the asparagus and mushrooms before the mushrooms start to brown, about 10 minutes.

4. Blend the artichoke core pieces into a bowl with all a mushroom/asparagus mix. Set aside.

5. Cut or split a tiny sourdough loaf into 1-inch bits. (My loaf was a little too small, therefore that I used 4 challah rolls too)

6. Grease a 9x13 inch baking dish and generate a base coating of bread at the dish. Spread 1/2 cup of Fontina cheese bread, at a coating, and disperse half an apple mixture on the cheese.

7. Lay-down a different layer of these vegetables and bread and high using a 1/2 cup of Fontina cheese.

8. Whisk together eggs, salt, milk, dry mustard, and pepper into a bowl, and then pour the egg mixture on the vegetables and bread.

9. Cover the dish, and then simmer for 3 weeks.

10. Pre Heat oven to 375 degrees.

11. Eliminate the casserole from the fridge and let stand for half an hour.

12. Spread All the Parmesan cheese at a coating within the strata.

13. Bake in the preheated oven until a time when a knife inserted near the border comes out clean, 40 to 45 minutes. Allow it stand 5 to 10 minutes before cutting into squares.

20. Almond Butter Granola

Ingredients

- 3 Cups of rolled oat
- 1 cup of almonds, sliced
- 1/3 cup of shredded coconut
- One and a half cup hemp seeds
- 1 cinnamon ground teaspoon
- 1/4 cubit kosher salt
- One and a half cup creamy almond butter
- A 1/4 cup of melted coconut oil
- 1/4 tablespoon maple syrup to taste

Directions

1. Preheat the oven to 300 ° F. Line a silicone matted baking sheet or gently mist with a baking spray.

2. Stir together the oats, almonds, coconut, hemp seeds, cinnamon, and salt in a big cup.

3. Whisk the almond butter, oil, and maple syrup together in a small cup. Pour the sauce over the oat mixture, then stir until coated evenly.

4. Spread the mixture into the baking tray ready and put it in the oven. Bake for about 20 minutes, then stir every 5 minutes.

5. When toasted, remove the granola from the oven and allow it to cool on a wire rack.

6. Break into smaller pieces when it's cold, and put in an airtight jar.

7. Enjoy yourself with yogurt, milk, or just a handful!

21. Egg White Veggie Wontons W/Fontina Topped W/ Crispy Prosciutto

Ingredients

- 1 cup egg whites

- Butter

- Fontina cheese

- Mixed shredded cheddar cheese

- Broccoli I utilized wheat, chopped bits

- Tomatoes - diced

- Salt and pepper

- Prosciutto - two pieces

Directions

1. Remove wonton wrappers out of the freezer.

2. Preheat the oven to 350.

3. Spray miniature cupcake tin with cooking spray.

4. After wrappers begin to defrost, peel off them carefully - apart, one at a time and press cupcake tin lightly.

5. I sliced the wrappers having a little bit of peanut butter. (optional)

6. Set a chunk of cheese in every bottom.

7. Satisfy desired lettuce - I used pre-cooked broccoli bits and diced tomatoes.

8. Pour egg whites all toppings.

9. Sprinkle each with some of those shredded cheddar cheese.

10. Cook for approximately 15 minutes, but get started watching them afterward 10 - whenever they poof up - assess them poking the middle with a fork.

11. While eggs are cooking, then spray a sheet of foil with cooking spray and then put 2 pieces of prosciutto onto it and then cook at exactly the exact same period as the egg whites. After 8 minutes, then take and let sit once it cools it becomes crispy and chop and high eggs!

Chapter 2. Pescatarian Lunch Recipes

1. Salmon with Blueberries

Ingredients

- 10-ounce Fillet Salmon

- 1/2 yellow medium onion, diced

- 1 cup of white wine

- 1 1/2 tablespoons vinegar for white wine

- 1 stick of cinnamon

- 1 cup blueberries

- 2 spoonfuls of butter

- 1 pound of honey

- 4 cups mixed greens

Directions

2. Remove the salmon from the freezer, and sprinkle with salt. Preheat the oven to 200 C (400 degrees F).

3. In a medium-sized pot, mix the onion, white wine, vinegar, and cinnamon stick and bring to a simmer over low heat. Cook for 10 minutes, it is enough to evaporate much of the liquid.

4. Add the blueberries, butter, and honey to the wine mixture and cook for 3 to 5 minutes or until dark pink is in the blueberries.

5. In a baking dish, put the salmon and cover with the blueberry mixture. For 8 minutes, bake.

6. Attach a large plate of mixed greens, drizzle with a few tablespoons of blueberry sauce, and top with salmon and blueberries.

7. Serve forthwith.

2. Miso-Marinated Baked Cod with Sesame and Stir-Fried Greens

Ingredients

- 3 1⁄2 teaspoons (20 g) miso

- 1 tablespoon mirin

- 1 tablespoon extra-virgin olive oil

- 1 x 7-ounce (200 g) skinless cod fillet

- 1⁄8 cup (20 g) red onion, sliced

- 3⁄8 cup (40 g) celery, sliced

- 2 cloves of garlic, finely chopped

- 1 Thai chili, finely chopped

- 1 teaspoon of fresh ginger

- 3⁄8 cup (60 g) green beans

- 3⁄4 cup (50 g) kale, roughly chopped

Directions

1. Rub the cod all over, and leave for 30 minutes to marinate. Heat the oven to 220 ° C (425oF).

2. Bake the cod for about 10 minutes.

3. Meanwhile, heat the remaining oil to a large frying pan or wok. Stir-fry the onion for a few minutes, then add the celery, garlic, chili, ginger, green beans, and kale. Toss and fry until the kale is cooked through and tender. To help the cooking process, you might need to add a little water to the pan.

4. Cook the buckwheat along with the turmeric according to the package instructions.

5. To the stir-fry, add the sesame seeds, parsley, and tamari and serve with buckwheat and shrimp.

3. Salmon Salad Niçoise

Ingredients

- 2 Spoonfuls of olive oil, divided

- 1/2 pound of fresh, quartered baby potatoes

- 8-10 carrots

- 2 Salmon fillets

- 3 hard-boiled, halved eggs

- 1/3 cup blended olives

- 1/2 cup of tomatoes with cherry, halved

- 5-8 strawberries

- 10 hearts of artichokes, halved

- 3 cups of arugula

- Optional-edible flowers for garnishing

- 1/4 cup of olive oil

- 1 tbsp. mustard whole grain

- 1 spoonful of apple cider vinegar

- A pinch of pepper and salt

Directions

1. Heat oven to 232 C (450 degrees F).

2. Attach the potatoes and carrots to a roasting pan or baking sheet. Sprinkle with olive oil and apply salt and pepper.

3. Bake for 20-30 minutes or until softened with a fork.

4. Heat a pan over medium to high heat. Drizzle the olive oil with the salmon fillets and sprinkle with salt and pepper.

5. Place the salmon (skin side up) in the pan when the pan is hot, and cook for 4-5 minutes or until golden brown on one side.

6. Flip over the salmon and cook for 3 more minutes or until the skin is crispy. The salmon, with an instant-read thermometer, should be 145 degrees F in the middle.

7. Combine all the egg-to-arugula ingredients on a large platter and top with the salmon, carrots, and potatoes.

8. Combine all the ingredients for the dressing (olive oil, mustard, vinegar, salt, and pepper) and whisk together briskly.

9. Using dressing and edible flowers to top the salad.

4. Salmon and Vegetable Quinoa

Ingredients

- 1 Cup, uncooked quinoa

- 1⁄2 tsp. kosher salt

- 3⁄4 Cup English cucumbers, seeded, diced

- 1 cup of cherry tomatoes, half-sliced

- 1⁄4 cup of red onion, thinly diced

- 4 thin-sliced basil leaves

- One lemon's zest

Salmon

- 1⁄2 tsp. kosher salt

- 1⁄4 black pepper teaspoon

- 1 tsp. cumin

- 1⁄2 tsp. paprika

- 20 Ounces of fillets for salmon, (four bits of 5 ounces)

- 8 wedges of lemon

- 1⁄4 cup parsley, freshly chopped

Directions

1. Bring 1 cup quinoa, 2 cups of water, and 1/2 teaspoon salt to a boil in a medium-sized saucepan with a lid.

2. Cover and simmer, cook for about 20 minutes, or as directed in the packet until the quinoa is light and fluffy.

3. Switch off the heat and let it sit before serving for at least 5 minutes.

4. Mix the cucumbers, tomatoes, onions, basil, and lemon zest shortly before serving. In the meantime, make your salmon.

5. Combine the salt, pepper, cumin, and paprika in a small cup.

6. Line a sheet pan or glass dish with foil and grate lightly with olive oil or non-stick spray.

7. Move the salmon fillets to the pan and evenly coat each filet's surface with around 1/2 teaspoon of the spice mix.

8. Place the wedges with the lemon at the edges of the pan.

9. Broil for 8 to 10 minutes on high with the rack put in the lower third of the oven, or until salmon is cooked and easily flakes apart with a fork.

10. Sprinkle with parsley and serve with wedges of roasted lemon and quinoa for vegetables.

5. Sticky Chicken Water Melon Noodle Salad

Ingredients

- 2 pieces of skinny rice noodles

- 1/2 tbsp. sesame oil

- 2 cups Water Melon

- Head of bib lettuce

- Half of a Lot of scallions

- Half of a Lot of fresh cilantro

- 2 skinless, boneless chicken breasts

- 1/2 tbsp. Chinese five-spice

- 1 tbsp. extra virgin olive oil

- two tbsp. sweet skillet (I utilized a mixture of maple syrup using a dash of Tabasco)

- 1 tbsp. sesame seeds

- a couple of cashews - smashed

- Dressing - could be made daily or 2 until

- 1 tbsp. low-salt soy sauce

- 1 teaspoon sesame oil

- 1 tbsp. peanut butter

- Half of a refreshing red chili

- Half of a couple of chives

- Half of a couple of cilantro

- Inch limes - juiced

- 1 small spoonful of garlic

Directions

1. In a bowl, completely submerge the noodles in boiling water. They will be ready in 2 minutes.

2. On a big sheet of parchment paper, then throw the chicken with pepper, salt, and also the five-spice.

3. Fold the paper, then pound and flatten the chicken with a rolling pin.

4. Place it into the large skillet with 1 tbsp. of olive oil, turning 3 or 4 minutes, until well charred and cooked through.

5. Drain the noodles and toss them with 1 tbsp. of sesame oil onto a sizable serving dish.

6. Place 50% of the noodles into the moderate skillet, stirring frequently until crispy and nice.

7. Eliminate the Watermelon skin, then slice the flesh to inconsistent balls and then increase the platter.

8. Reduce the lettuces and cut into small wedges and also half of a whole lot of leafy greens and scatter the dish.

9. Place the other half of the cilantro pack, the soy sauce, coriander, chives, peanut butter, and a dab of water, 1 teaspoon of sesame oil, and the lime juice then mix till smooth.

10. Set the chicken back to heat, garnish with all the sweet skillet (or my walnut syrup mixture), and toss with the sesame seeds.

11. Pour the dressing on the salad toss gently with fresh fingers until well coated, then add crispy noodles and then smashed cashews.

12. Blend chicken pieces and add them to the salad.

6. Roasted Eggplant and Shrimp with Harissa

Ingredients

- 1 big eggplant, cut into 1-inch pieces

- 1/3 cup + 1 tbs. olive oil

- 2 tsp. harissa

- 1 1/2 tsp. cumin

- 2 tsp. salt

- 12 oz. Shrimp shelled and deveined

- 1/2 tsp. cumin seeds

- 1 teaspoon zest of lemon

- 1 freshly ground teaspoon of black pepper

- 1 tablespoon of lemon juice that has been freshly squeezed

- 1/4 cup of fresh mint finely chopped

Directions

1. The oven should be preheated to 400 degrees F

2. Whisk together 1/3 of a cup of olive oil, harissa, cumin, and 1 teaspoon of salt in a small bowl.

3. Spread the eggplant over a large baking sheet with rims. Drizzle with a mixture of harissa, then toss to cover it. Spread the eggplant so that there are bits in a single sheet.

4. 20 Minutes to roast eggplant.

5. Meanwhile, blend the shrimp, 1 1/2 tablespoons of oil, cumin seeds, lemon zest, remaining salt, and pepper in a large bowl.

6. On another rimmed baking sheet, lay out the shrimp.

7. Heat up the oven to 425 degrees F and add the shrimp to the oven. Turn the tray 180 degrees and toss the eggplant.

8. Leave both trays in the oven for between 7 and 10 minutes. When they are a little white in colour and they have developed a C shape, the shrimp will be done. They should be 165 degrees F on an instant-read thermometer. The eggplant is finished when it's browned.

9. Combine the shrimp and eggplant with lemon juice and mint on a large platter and top. Serve forthwith.

7. Baked Lemon Dill Salmon

Ingredients

- 2 6-8 ounce fillets of salmon (organic, wild if you can find them!)

- 1 bunch of fresh dill, washed dry and patted

- Two Citrons

- 1/2 tsp. Salt

- 1 new teaspoon of pepper

Directions

1. Preheat the furnace to 375 F.

2. Juice a lemon into a tiny bowl and set aside. Break the remaining lemon into around 1/4 inch thick rounds.

3. Line the aluminium foil on a baking sheet and put the fillets on the skin side down.

4. Sprinkle the lemon juice over the filets and season with salt and pepper.

5. Drape the fillets with the fresh dill sprigs-be generous as you just want to cover the dill with the salmon so that the taste soaks in.

6. Cover with wedges of lemon.

7. Bake the salmon until the salmon is completely cooked, for around 20 minutes.

8. Take off the oven, and serve!

8. Asian Shrimp Stir-Fry with Buckwheat Noodles

Ingredients

- 1/ pound (150 g) shelled raw jumbo shrimp, deveined

- 2 teaspoons tamari (or soy sauce, if you don't want gluten)

- 2 teaspoons extra virgin olive oil

- 3 ounces (75 g) soba (buckwheat noodles)

- 2 garlic cloves, nicely chopped

- 1 Thai chili, nicely chopped

- 1 teaspoon nicely chopped fresh ginger

- 1/cup (20 g) red onions, sliced

- 1/cup (45 g) celery including leaves, trimmed and cut, with leaves mounted.

Directions

1. Load the shrimp onto a tray. Wipe the pan out with a towel of ink, because you will be using it again.

2. Cook the noodles for 5 to 8 minutes in boiling water, or as indicated on the box. Drain and put away.

3. Meanwhile, in the remaining tamari and oil over medium-high heat, fry the garlic, chili, ginger, red onion, celery (but not the leaves), green beans, and kale for 2 to 3 min. Add the stock and allow to a boil, then cook for a minute or two until cooked but crunchy.

4. Add the shrimp, noodles, and leaves of celery to the pan, bring back to a boil, then remove and serve from heat.

9. Orange Salmon and Lentils

Ingredients

- 2 (4 to 6 ounces) fillet salmon

- 3 Cara Cara Oranges

- 2 spoonfuls of brown sugar

- 1 bag of Swiss chard or rainbow chard

- 2 cups of lentils cooked brown or green

- Pinch salt and pepper

- Microgreens-optional topping

Directions

1. Preheat the oven to 425 degrees F

2. In a cup, mix the juice of one orange Cara Cara, brown sugar, a pinch of salt and pepper, and whisk together.

3. Pat the filets dry with salmon. Drizzle over the fillets with half the orange juice mixture, reserving the remainder for later.

4. Roast the salmon for 6 to 8 minutes, or until it flakes easily with a fork or reads 145 degrees F on a thermometer read-in.

5. In a large skillet heat the olive oil, and cook the chard until wilted. With a pinch of salt and pepper, season.

6. Cut in rounds of the remaining oranges. On each plate, put half the oranges, chard, lentils, and a salmon fillet. Drizzle and serve immediately with the remaining orange juice.

10. Pecan Crusted Salmon

Ingredients

- 1/2 cup of quinoa, uncooked
- 1 cup of vegetable broth
- 1/8 cup fine-cut parsley
- 1/8 cup of crumbs with panko bread
- 1/8 cup of shredded pecans
- A pinch of pepper and salt
- 2 chunks of salmon
- 1 tbsp. of butter
- 1 tbsp. honey
- 1 tbsp. of soy sauce
- 1 tbsp. of lemon juice
- 1 tsp. ginger rubbed
- 1/2 tsp. corn-starch

Directions

1. Preheat oven to 400 F.

2. Mix the uncooked quinoa and the broth in a medium saucepan and cook according to the box. (I only cook my quinoa until all the liquid is gone, stirring regularly, and sometimes adding a few more spoonfuls of water/broth if the quinoa is not finished yet).

3. While the quinoa is cooking, prepare the breading by adding to a food processor and grinding the parsley, bread crumbs, pecans, and salt & pepper, until thoroughly combined. That should only take about 15 seconds of processing.

4. In the bread crumb mixture, dredge each of the salmon parts so that the salmon is completely coated.

5. Melt the butter over medium heat in a skillet. Add in the salmon and sear for about 1 minute on each side. Put the whole skillet in the oven until all sides are seared and bake for 10-12 minutes.

6. Make the sauce by whisking together the sugar, soy sauce, lemon juice, corn starch, and grated ginger while the quinoa finishes and the salmon bakes.

7. Once quinoa and salmon have been done and slightly cooled, plate the quinoa evenly on 2 plates and top with the salmon. Dissolve the honey sauce uniformly over the salmon.

11. Miso and Sesame Glazed Tofu

Ingredients

- 1 tbsp. mirin

- 3 1/2tsp. (20 g) miso paste

- 1 x 5-ounce (150 g) block of tofu

- 1 stalk (40 g) celery, trimmed (about 1/cup when sliced)

- 1/4 cup (40 g) red onion, sliced

- 1 tiny (120 g) zucchini (about 1 cup when sliced)

- 1 Thai chili

- 2 garlic cloves

- 1 tsp. of nicely chopped fresh ginger

- 3/4 cup (50 g) kale, chopped

- 2 tsp. sesame seeds

- 1/4 cup (35 g) buckwheat

- 1 tsp. ground turmeric

- 1 tsp. extra virgin olive oil

- 1 tsp. tamari

Directions

1. Heat the oven to 400 F. Line a thin, parchment-paper roasting pan.

2. Mix in the mirin and the miso. Lengthwise cut the tofu, then diagonally cut each piece into triangles in half. Fill the tofu with the miso mix and leave to marinate while the other ingredients are prepared.

3. Slice the angle into the celery, red onion, and zucchini. Chop the chili, garlic, and ginger thinly, then set aside.

4. Let the Kale for 5 minutes in a steamer. Discard and set aside.

5. Place the tofu in the roasting pan, sprinkle the tofu with the sesame seeds, and roast in the oven for 15 to 20 minutes until it has been beautifully caramelized.

6. Wash the buckwheat in a sieve, then place it along with the turmeric in a saucepan of boiling water. Cook as indicated by a box, then drain.

7. Heat the oil in a frying pan; add the celery, onion, zucchini, chili, garlic, and ginger and fry over high heat for 1 to 2 minutes, then reduce to medium heat for 3 to 4 minutes until the vegetables are cooked through, but are still crunchy. If the vegetables begin to stick to the pan, you can need to add a tablespoon of water. Add the tamari and kale, and cook for another minute.

8. Serve with the greens and buckwheat, when the tofu is finished.

12. Poached Sea Bass

Ingredients

- 1 spoonful of butter

- 1/2 yellow onion, sliced thinly

- 2 fillets of sea bass

- 1 dried oregano teaspoon

- Flakes of 1 teaspoon of red pepper

- 1 salt teaspoon

- 1 cup of white wine

- 2 Roma tomatoes, cut into slices

- 10 Olives from Castelvetrano, halved

- Parsley 1/4 cup, coarsely chopped

- 1/4 cup, coarsely chopped basil

Directions

1. Heat the butter over medium-high heat in a large skillet.

2. Stir in the onions and sauté for 4 to 5 minutes, or until translucent.

3. Place the fish with oregano, red pepper flakes, and salt on top of the onions.

4. Nestle then in the tomatoes, and pour in the wine.

5. Cover and simmer until the fish is finished, or 6 minutes.

6. Put the olives, parsley, and basil on top and serve.

13. Kale and Red Onion Dhal with Buckwheat

Ingredients

- 1 tbsp. coconut oil

- 1 small red onion, chopped

- 3 Garlic cloves, crushed or grated

- 2 Cm lemon, grated

- 1 Birdseye chili, deseeded and finely chopped (more if you like things sexy!)

- 2 tsp. turmeric

- 2 tsp. garam masala

- 160g Red lentils

- 400ml Coconut milk

- 200ml Water

- 100g Kale (or lettuce are a terrific alternative)

- 160g buckwheat (or brown rice)

Directions

1. Put the coconut oil in a large, deep saucepan, and then add the chopped onion. Cook on very low heat, with the lid for five minutes until softened.

2. Insert the ginger, garlic, and chili and cook 1 minute.

3. Insert the garlic, garam masala, and a dash of water, and then cook for 1 minute.

4. Insert The reddish peas, coconut milk, and also 200ml water (try so only by half filling the coconut milk could with water and stirring it in the saucepan)

5. Mix everything together thoroughly and then cook for 20 minutes over lightly heat with the lid. Stir occasionally and add just a little bit more water in case the dhal starts to stand.

6. Later 20 seconds add the carrot, stir thoroughly and then replace the lid, then cook for a further five minutes (1 2 minutes if you are using spinach)

7. Around 1-5 minutes ahead of the curry is ready, set the buckwheat at a medium saucepan, and then put in lots of warm water. Bring back the water to the boil and then cook for 10 minutes (or only a little longer in case you would rather your buckwheat softer. Drain the buckwheat at a sieve and function with the dhal.

14. Char-grilled Steak

Ingredients

- 5g parsley, finely chopped

- 100g potatoes, peeled and cut into 2cm dice

- 50g Lettuce, chopped

- 1 tbsp. extra virgin coconut oil

- 50g Red onion, chopped into circles

- 1 garlic clove, finely chopped

- 120--150g 3.5cm-thick beef noodle beef or 2cm-thick sirloin beef

- 40ml Red wine

- 150ml Beef inventory

- 1 tsp. tomato purée

- 1 tsp. corn flour, dissolved in 1 tablespoon water

Directions

1. Heat the oven to 220ºC.

2. Put the sausage in a saucepan of boiling water, then return to the boil and then cook 4minutes, then empty.

3. Put in a skillet with 1 tbsp. of the oil and then roast in the oven for 3-5 --4-5 minutes. Twist the berries every 10 minutes to ensure even cooking.

4. After cooking, remove from the oven, sprinkle with the chopped parsley, and mix well.

5. Fry the onion 1 tsp. of the oil over a moderate heat for 5 minutes --1 minute, until tender and well caramelized. Maintain heat. Steam the kale for two-three minutes.

6. Stir the garlic lightly in 1/2 tsp. of oil for 1 minute, until tender but not colored.

7. Insert the spinach and simmer for a further 1--two minutes, until tender. Maintain heat.

8. Heating an ovenproof skillet on high heat until smoking.

9. Lay the beef from 1/2 a tsp. of the oil and then fry from the skillet over a moderate-high temperature in accordance with just how you would like your beef done. If you prefer your beef moderate, it'd be wise to sear the beef and also transfer the pan into a toaster place in 220ºC/petrol 7 and then finish the cooking which manner to your prescribed occasions.

10. Remove the meat from the pan and put aside to break. Add your wine into the skillet to bring any meat up residue. Bubble to decrease the wine by half an hour until syrupy, along with a flavour that is concentrated.

11. Insert the inventory and tomato purée into the beef pan and bring to the boil, add the cornflour paste to thicken your sauce, then adding it only a little at a time till you've got your preferred consistency. Stir in just about anyone of those juices out of the dinner that is rested and serve with the roasted lettuce, celery, onion rings, and red berry sauce.

15. Grilled Shrimp and Endives

Ingredients

- 4 to 6 Belgian endives

- 1 tbsp. olive oil

- 1 pound of shrimp, deveined and washed

- 4 tsp. Pesto

- Salt, only to taste

- 3 cups of greens

- 1/4 cup parmesan, shredded

- 1 litter, olive oil

Directions

1. Heat the grilling pan until very hot over medium-high heat.

2. Break the endives in half and sprinkle with 1 spoonful of olive oil. Put them into the plate. Cook 3 minutes on each side of the endives.

3. In a cup, mix the shrimp and pesto, and whisk until the shrimp is fully coated.

4. After the endives have cooked, put the shrimp in the grill pan and cook for 1 to 2 minutes on each side until the shrimp is pink and curled.

5. Either serve the shrimp and endive alone or put greens on a plate or wooden cutting board, cover with olive oil and half the parmesan.

6. Add the shrimp and endives to the pan, and cover half the parmesan with the other.

7. Serve forthwith.

16. Baked Potatoes with Spicy Chickpea Stew

Ingredients

- 4- 6 Celery, pricked all over
- 2 tsp. coconut oil
- 2 Red onions, finely chopped
- 4 cloves of garlic, crushed or grated
- 2cm ginger, grated
- 1/2 -2 teaspoons chili flakes (depending on how hot you enjoy stuff)
- 2 tbsp. cumin seeds
- 2 tsp. turmeric
- Splash of water
- 2 x 400g tins chopped tomatoes
- 2 tbsp. unsweetened cocoa powder (or even cacao)
- 2 X 400g tins chickpeas including the chick-pea water, do not DRAIN!!
- 2 Yellow peppers (or any colour you would like!), chopped into bite-size pieces
- 2 tbsp. parsley and extra for garnish
- Salt And pepper to taste (optional)

Directions

1. Pre Heat The oven to 200C, however, you are able to prepare all of your own ingredients.

2. When the oven is still hot enough to set your lemon potatoes from the oven and cook for 1 hour or so until they do the way you prefer them.

3. Once The potatoes come from the oven, then place the coconut oil and sliced red onion into a large wide saucepan and cook lightly, with the lid for five minutes until the onions are tender but not brown.

4. Remove the lid and then add the ginger, garlic, cumin, and simmer.

5. Cook for a further minute on very low heat, then add the garlic and a tiny dab of water and then cook for another moment; just take care never to allow the pan to get too tender.

6. Next, Add from the berries, cocoa powder (or even cacao), chickpeas (including the chickpea water), and salt.

7. Allow to boil, and then simmer on a very low heat for 4-5 seconds before the sauce is thick and unctuous (but do not allow it to burn up).

8. The stew ought to be performed at exactly the exact same period as the legumes.

9. Finally, Stir at the two tbsp. of parsley, plus a few pepper and salt if you desire, and also serve the stew in addition to the chopped sausage, possibly with a very simple salad.

17. Blackened Tilapia Salad

Ingredients

- 4 tilapia fillets

- 3 tbsp. of butter or lard, split

- 3 tsp. Seasoning old bay

- 6 cups romaine lettuce (1 heart), chopped

- 1/4 red cabbage, sliced

- 1/2 cup of cilantro

- 2 avocado, shredded

- From 2 limes, zest, optional

- 8 tbsp. Lemon Chesapeake dressing with Tessemae

Directions

1. Toss the Romaine, the cabbage, and the coriander together in a large salad bowl.

2. Melt 2 tablespoons of the fat and coat the fillets deeply in fat.

3. Sprinkle over the seasoning generously on both sides of the fillets.

4. It should be seasoned more heavily than you normally season fish.

5. In a medium skillet over medium-high heat, melt another tablespoon of fat.

6. Fry the tilapia fillets in the skillet for about 3 minutes on each side when it is light, or until slightly blackened, and the fish is completely cooked.

7. To trap excess fat place fish on a paper towel. Top with lime zest.

8. Serve the salad on top with sliced tilapia and sliced avocado, then drizzle with the dressing for the salad.

18. Lamb, Butternut Squash and Date Tagine

Ingredients

- 2 tsp. coconut oil

- 1 red onion, chopped

- 2cm ginger, grated

- 3 garlic cloves, crushed or grated

- 1 tsp. chili flakes (or to taste)

- 2 tsp. cumin seeds

- 2 tsp. ground turmeric

- 1 cinnamon stick

- 800g lamb neck fillet, cut into 2cm chunks

- 1/2 tsp. salt

- 100g Medjool dates, pitted and sliced

- 400g Tin chopped berries, and half of a can of plain water

- 500g Butternut squash, chopped into 1cm cubes

- 400g Tin chickpeas, drained

- 2 tsp. fresh coriander (and extra for garnish)

- Buckwheat, Couscous, flatbread, or rice to function

Directions

1. Preheat your oven to 140C.

2. Drizzle Roughly 2 tbsp. of coconut oil into a large ovenproof saucepan or cast-iron casserole dish. Add the chopped onion and cook on a gentle heat, with the lid for around five minutes, until the onions are softened but not too brown.

3. Insert The grated ginger and garlic, chili, cumin, cinnamon, and garlic. Stir well and cook 1 minute with off the lid.

4. Add a dash of water when it becomes too humid.

5. Next, add from the lamb balls.

6. Stir to coat the beef from the spices and onions, then add the salt chopped meats and berries and roughly half of a can of plain water (100-200ml).

7. Place the tagine into the boil and put the lid and put on the skillet for about 1 hour and fifteen minutes.

8. Ten minutes before the conclusion of this cooking period, add the chopped butternut squash and drained chickpeas.

9. Stir everything together, place the lid back and go back to the oven for the last half an hour of cooking.

10. When the tagine is able to remove from the oven and then stir fry throughout the chopped coriander. Drink buckwheat, couscous, flatbread, or basmati rice.

19. Prawn Arrabbiata

Ingredients

- 125-150 g beef or cooked prawns (Ideally king prawns)

- 65g Buckwheat pasta

- 1 tbsp. extra virgin coconut oil

Arrabbiata Sauce

- 40 g red onion, finely chopped

- 1 garlic clove, finely chopped

- 30g celery, thinly sliced

- 1 bird's eye chili, finely chopped

- 1 tsp. dried mixed veggies

- 1 tsp. extra virgin coconut oil

- 2 tbsp. white wine (optional)

- 400g tinned chopped berries

- 1 tbsp. Chopped parsley

Directions

1. Fry the garlic, onion, celery, and peppermint and peppermint blossoms in the oil over moderate-low heat for 1--2 weeks.

2. Turn up the heat to medium, bring the wine and cook 1 second. Add the berries and leave the sauce simmer over moderate-low heat for 20--half an hour, until it's a great rich texture.

3. In the event you're feeling that the sauce is becoming too thick, simply put in just a very little water.

4. As the sauce is cooking, attract a bowl of water to the boil and then cook the pasta as per the package directions.

5. Once cooked to your dish, drain, then toss with the olive oil and also maintain at the pan before needed.

6. If you're utilizing raw prawns, put them into your sauce and cook for a further 3--four minutes, till they've turned opaque and pink, then add the parsley and function.

7. If you're using cooked prawns, insert them using the skillet, then bring the sauce to the boil, and then function.

8. Add the cooked pasta into the sauce, then mix thoroughly but lightly and function.

20. Turmeric Baked Salmon

Ingredients

- 125-150g skinned salmon
- 1 tsp. extra virgin coconut oil
- 1 tsp. ground turmeric
- 1/4 cup lemon juice

Hot Celery

- 1 tsp. extra virgin coconut oil
- 40g red onion, finely chopped
- 60g tinned green peas
- 1 garlic clove, finely chopped
- 1 cm fresh ginger, finely chopped
- 1 bird's eye chili, finely chopped
- 150g celery, cut into 2cm lengths
- 1 tsp. darkened curry powder
- 130g tomato, cut into 8 wedges
- 100ml vegetable or pasta stock
- 1 tbsp. parsley, chopped

Directions

1. Heat the oven to 200C / gas mark 6.

2. Start using the hot celery. Heat a skillet over a moderate --low heat, then add the olive oil then the garlic, onion, ginger, celery, and peppermint.

3. Fry lightly for two-three minutes until softened but not colored, you can add the curry powder and cook for a further minute.

4. Insert the berries afterward, your lentils and stock, and simmer for 10 seconds.

5. You might choose to increase or reduce the cooking time according to how crunchy you'd like your own sausage.

6. Meanwhile, mix the garlic olive oil and lemon juice and then rub the salmon.

7. Set on the baking dish and cook 8--10 seconds.

8. In order to complete, stir the skillet throughout the celery and function with the salmon.

21. Spinach and Feta Stuffed Salmon

Ingredients

- 2 Spoonfuls of olive oil, divided

- 4 (6-ounces) fillets of salmon

- 1 yellow medium onion, diced

- 2 Garlic cloves, minced

- 3 Cups Children's Spinach

- 1/3 Cup Feta Crumbled

- 1 tbsp Kosher salt

- Microgreens-optional topping-

Directions

1. Preheat the oven to 200 C (400 degrees F).

2. Heat 1 tablespoon of olive oil over medium to high heat in a large skillet.

3. Sauté for 3 to 4 minutes with the onions and garlic or until the onions are translucent.

4. Attach the spinach and cook until wilted, or for 30 seconds. Take the pan off the heat and whisk in the feta.

5. Flip the salmon filets to their side and cut through them lengthwise to create a pocket.

6. Divide the spinach mixture into four equal parts and stock each fillet with salmon.

7. Drizzle the remaining olive oil to the fillets. Bake the fillets for 8 to 10 minutes on a rimmed cookie sheet, or until the salmon flakes apart.

22. Poke Bowls with Ahi Tuna

Ingredients

- Ahi tuna, 1 pound sushi, cut into 3/4-inch cubes

- A half cup of soy sauce 1/4 cup of soy sauce

- 1 tsp. vinegar for rice

- 1 1/2 tsp. sesame oil

- 3/4 tsp. flakes of red pepper, crushed

- 1/3 Cup of green onions, with thin slices

- 1/2 tsp. sesame seeds, with garnishing

- 2 cups of cooked brown rice, or cooked white rice

- 2 cups of greens for salad

Directions

1. Wash the rice under running water, and cook it, as instructed by the manufacturer.

2. Ahi tuna, soy sauce, rice vinegar, sesame oil, crushed red pepper flakes, green onions, and sesame seeds are mixed in a medium-sized dish.

3. Serve immediately or refrigerate up to 2 hours before serving, sealed. Until serving, toss in the sauce to recombine.

4. In each bowl, add the cooked rice, salad, poke, and desired toppings.

24. Baked Salmon Salad with Creamy Mint Dressing

Ingredients

- 1 Salmon Shrimp (130g)
- 40g Mixed salad leaves
- 40g young spinach leaves
- 2 Radishes, trimmed and thinly chopped
- 5cm slice (50g) cucumber, cut into balls
- 2 Spring onions, trimmed and chopped
- 1 Small number (10g) parsley, roughly sliced

Dressing

- 1 tsp. low-fat mayonnaise
- 1 tbsp. organic yogurt
- 1 tbsp. rice vinegar
- 2 Leaves mint, finely chopped
- Salt And freshly ground black pepper

Directions

1. Preheat the oven to 200°C (180°C fan/Gas 6).
2. Set the salmon fillet onto a baking dish and bake for 16--18 minutes until cooked.
3. Remove from the oven and place aside.
4. The salmon is every bit as fine cold or hot in the salad. If your poultry contains skin, then just brush down the skin and eliminate the salmon out of the skin by means of a fish piece after ingestion. It will slide easily once cooked.
5. In a small bowl, add the mayonnaise, yogurt, rice vinegar, coriander leaves, and salt and salt together and leave to stand for at least 5 minutes to permit the tastes to grow.
6. Arrange the salad lettuce and leaves onto the serving plate and top with the radishes, cucumber, spring onions, and parsley.

7. Flake the carrot on the salad and drizzle the dressing.

25. Choc Processor Granola

Ingredients

- 200g jumbo oats
- 50g pecans, chopped
- 3 tbsps. Olive oil
- 20g Butter
- 1 tbsp. dark brown sugar
- 2 tbsps. Rice malt syrup
- 60g Good-quality (70 percent) Darkened Chocolate chips

Directions

1. Preheat the oven to 160°C. Line a large baking dish having a baking parchment or silicone sheet.

2. Combine the oats and pecans together in a huge bowl.

3. At a modest skillet, gently warm the coconut oil, butter, brown sugar, and rice malt butter before the butter has melted, and the sugar and butter have simmered.

4. Don't let it boil. Pour the syrup on the ginger and stir thoroughly before the oats are wholly covered.

5. Distribute the granola within the skillet, dispersing straight into the corners.

6. Leave clumps of mix with spacing as opposed to an additional disperse.

7. Bake in the oven for about 20 minutes before only tinged gold-brown at the edges.

8. Remove from the oven and allow it to cool to the menu altogether.

9. If cool, divide some larger lumps onto the plate together with your palms and mix in the chocolate chips.

10. Twist or put the granola in an airtight jar or tub.

11. The granola will keep for a minimum of two weeks.

Chapter 3. Pescatarian Dinner Recipes

1. Bang Bang Shrimp Pasta

Ingredients

- For the crispy breadcrumbs:

- Unsalted butter for 1 tablespoon

- 1/2 cup fresh breadcrumbs or Panko

- 1/8 tsp. of kosher salt

- 1/8 teaspoon of black pepper, freshly ground

- Cayenne pepper with a pinch

- Garlic powder pinch

- Kitchen spray

- 1/2 cup plain Greek yogurt with whole milk

- 2 Tablespoons of Asian chili-garlic sauce, for example, sambal oelek

- 1 honey teaspoon

- 1/4 cup of garlic powder

- 2 medium limes (approximately 1/4 cup) of juice, divided

- 12 Untitled dry spaghetti

- 1 pound of uncooked, peeled medium shrimp deveined

- 1/2 teaspoon kosher salt, plus water for pasta

- 1/4 teaspoon of black pepper, freshly ground

- 1/8 cayenne pepper teaspoon

- 2 medium scallions, sliced thinly, divided

Directions

1. Melt the butter over medium heat over a small skillet. Add the breadcrumbs, salt, black pepper, garlic powder, and cayenne pepper.

2. Cook, stirring constantly, for 4 to 5 minutes, until golden, crispy, and fragrant; set aside.

3. In the centre of the oven, position a rack and heat it to 400 ° F. Coat lightly with cooking spray on a rimmed baking sheet; set aside.

4. To a boil, put a big pot of salted water. Meanwhile, whisk in a small bowl together with the yogurt, chili-yellow sauce, sugar, garlic powder, and half the lime juice; set aside.

5. Add the pasta when the water is boiling, and cook until al dente, about 10 minutes, or as instructed by the packet.

6. Meanwhile, pat the shrimp dry and put on the baking sheet that has been prepared. Add the salt, black pepper, and cayenne to the seasoning and stir to cover.

7. Spread into a layer of evenness. Roast until the shrimp is opaque and pink, stirring halfway through once, total 6 to 8 minutes.

8. Drizzle over the shrimp and toss to cover the remaining lime juice, picking up any flavourful bits on the baking sheet.

9. Please drain the pasta and place it back in the pot. Pour in the sauce with yogurt and toss to cover the pasta evenly.

10. Along with half of the scallions, add the shrimp and any juices from the baking sheet and toss gently again.

11. The crispy breadcrumbs and remaining scallions are generously sprinkled on each serving. Serve forthwith.

2. Bacon and Egg Fried Rice Recipe

Ingredients

- 350g long-grain rice, well rinsed
- 1 $^1/_2$ tablespoon olive oil
- 100g streaky bacon, diced
- 2 peppers, finely chopped
- 2 red onions, finely chopped
- 200g carrots, peeled and coarsely grated
- 2 garlic cloves, crushed
- 5cm slice ginger, peeled and grated
- 1 red chili, finely chopped (optional)
- 2 eggs
- 2 tsp. soy sauce

Directions

1. Cook the rice in a big bowl of warm water for 10 mins until not quite tender. Drain, rinse with warm water, and drain. Set aside.

2. Meanwhile, warm 1/2 tablespoon oil in a skillet on high heat and fry the bacon for 5 7 mins until golden and crispy.

3. Remove from the pan using a slotted spoon and place aside. Add 1 tablespoon oil and fry the peppers for 10 mins until lightly bubbling.

4. Add the carrots, onions, ginger, garlic, and chili and fry over a moderate-high temperature for 5 mins more.

5. Insert the rice and bacon and simmer for 5 mins, stirring often.

6. Push the rice mix to a single side of this pan and then crack the eggs to the gap.

7. Beat the eggs with a wooden spoon, then stir throughout the rice.

8. Cook for 2 mins, then add the soy sauce and then remove from heat. Split between 4 shallow bowls to function.

3. Sheet Pan Honey-Sesame Tofu and Green Beans

Ingredients

- Extra-firm 12 ounces tofu, drained and patted dry
- Oil or mist for cooking
- 2 tablespoons of sodium-reduced soy sauce or tamari
- Garlic with 3 cloves, minced
- 1 Pound of honey
- 1 Tablespoon of fresh ginger
- 1 Teaspoon of heated sesame oil
- 1 pound of green, trimmed beans
- 2 tbsp. of olive oil
- 1/4 teaspoon flakes of red pepper (optional)
- Seasonal salt
- Freshly roasted black chili
- 1 Medium, thinly sliced scallion
- Sesame seeds 1/4 teaspoon

Directions

1. Cover a large plate with paper towels, and top with the tofu. Cover with more paper towels and top with a heavy object, pressing down onto the tofu.

2. Set 10-30 minutes aside. Meanwhile, in the middle of the oven, position a rack and heat it to 400 ° F.

3. Oil a baking sheet thinly or cover with cooking spray. In a wide cup, whisk together the soya sauce or tamari, garlic, sugar, ginger, and sesame oil; set aside.

4. Cut the tofu into triangles and put on one-half of the prepared baking sheet in a single layer. Drizzle with a combination of soy sauces.

5. Bake at the bottom for 12 to 13 minutes, until it gets golden brown.

6. Tofu flip. Place the green beans onto the other half of the baking sheet in a single layer.

7. Connect the olive oil and sprinkle with the red flakes of pepper; season with salt and pepper.

8. Return to the oven and bake until the second side of the tofu is golden-brown, 10 to 12 more minutes.

9. Sprinkle with the seeds of scallions and sesame and serve right away.

4. Full-of-veg Hash Recipe

Ingredients

- 750g potatoes, pared and grated

- 2 tablespoon olive oil

- 100g streaky bacon, roughly sliced

- 2 red onions, finely chopped

- 300g carrots, peeled and diced

- 2 courgettes, diced

- 2 garlic cloves, crushed

- 4 eggs

- 5g refreshing flat-leaf parsley, sliced

- 1 red chili, chopped (optional)

- 1/2 x 340g jar pickled red cabbage

Directions

5. Pre heats the oven to 220°C, buff 200°C.

6. Bring a bowl of soapy water to the boil and then simmer the potatoes for 5 mins, then drain and put aside.

7. Heat 1 tablespoon oil in a large, ovenproof skillet on high heat and fry the bacon for 5 mins until crispy.

8. Add the carrots, onions, courgettes, onions, and garlic; season and then cook for 5 mins.

9. Transfer the pan into the oven and bake for 25-30 mins before the veg is tender and gold.

10. Meanwhile, heat the remaining oil into a skillet on medium-high heating and fry the eggs 2-3 mins or until cooked to your liking.

11. Split the hash between two plates and top each with lettuce.

12. Scatter with parsley and simmer, then function with the pickled red cabbage onto both.

5. Mason Jar Tuna Niçoise

Ingredients

Dressing

- 1 1/2 teaspoons of vinegar for red wine
- 1 Clove of garlic, chopped
- 1/2 teaspoon mustard from Dijon
- 1 fillet of anchovy, coarsely chopped (optional)
- Olive oil for 3 tablespoons
- 1/4 cubit kosher salt

Salad

- 4 Unhesitating fresh potatoes
- 2 ounces of green, trimmed beans
- 1 Medium pruned tomato
- 1 (4-ounce) Can drain tuna packed in water
- 1 Egg hard-boiled
- 10 Nicoise Pitted Olives
- 6 Lettuce leaves of Boston, broken into bite-sized pieces

Directions

1. Make the vinaigrette: In a small bowl, put all the ingredients and whisk until the anchovy fillet is emulsified, breaking it up.

2. Make the salad: place the potatoes in a small casserole and cover with cold water and salt. Bring to a boil over high-medium sun.

3. Cook for 5 to 8 minutes, until the potatoes are tender and can be pierced easily with a knife.

4. With a slotted spoon, cut the potatoes and set aside to cool completely.

5. Return the water to a boil and use the same saucepan.

6. The green beans are introduced. Cook for around 2 minutes, until just tender.

7. Drain the beans, and set aside to completely cool.

8. Assemble the salad: Add the vinaigrette to a quarter-sized Mason jar at the bottom.

9. Put green beans onto the dressing.

10. Core the tomato and dice it, then spread over the green beans.

11. Bring the tuna to pieces with a fork and add to the pot.

12. The egg is quartered and added to the pot.

13. To the pot, add the olives.

14. Cut the potatoes into slices 1/2 inch thick, and add to the container.

15. Top with salad greens on the container. Seal until ready to feed, then refrigerate.

16. Load the jar into a wide bowl to serve, and toss to mix.

6. Rita's 'Rowdy' Enchiladas Recipe

Ingredients

- Two large chicken breasts (about 400g)

- 2 red peppers, thinly chopped

- 1 tablespoon olive oil

- 3/4 tsp. mild chili powder

- 1 1/2 tsp. ground cumin

- 3/4 tsp. smoked paprika

- 80g grated mozzarella

- 8 Plain Tortilla Wraps

- 65g ripe Cheddar, grated

- 10g fresh coriander, roughly sliced

Sauce

- 1 tablespoon olive oil

- 1/2 onion, finely chopped

- 2 tsp. cloves, crushed

- 500g tomato passata

- 1 tablespoon chipotle chili paste

- 400g tin black beans drained and rinsed

- 1/2 lime, juiced

Directions

1. Pre heats the oven to gas 5, 190°C, buff 170°C.

2. Set the chicken at a 20 x 30cm skillet with all the peppers olive oil, chili powder, cumin, and paprika.

3. Mix to coat, then cover with foil.

4. Roast for 25-30 mins before the chicken is cooked and tender with no pink meat remains.

5. Take out the chicken from the dish and then shred with two forks. Reserve in a bowl.

6. Meanwhile, make the sauce.

7. Heat the oil in a saucepan on a low heat and cook the garlic and onion for 10 mins.

8. Stir from the passata and chipotle chili glue; increase heat to moderate, bring to a simmer and cook for a further 10 mins, stirring periodically.

9. Bring the beans and carrot juice season.

10. Mix one-third of this sauce plus half of the mozzarella to the cultured broccoli and chicken.

11. To gather, spoon 4 tablespoons of this sauce in exactly the exact baking dish before.

12. Spoon a bit of the chicken mixture down the middle of each tortilla, roll up, and then put it from the dish.

13. Repeat with the tortillas and filling, then placing them alongside in order that they do not shatter. Pour the remaining sauce on the top and then scatter within the Cheddar and remaining mozzarella. Bake in the oven for 20-25 mins until the cheese has melted and begun to brownish. Scatter together with all the coriander to function.

7. Salmon Salad

Ingredients

- Olive oil for 1/4 cup

- 3 teaspoons vinegar for red wine

- 2 Tablespoons of freshly squeezed lemon juice (1 lemon juice)

- 1 Clove of garlic, chopped

- 3/4 dried oregano teaspoon

- 1/2 kosher salt teaspoon

- 1/4 teaspoon of black pepper, freshly ground

- 1/2 Small, thinly sliced red onion

- Hot water 1/4 cup

- 4 (6-ounce) fillets of salmon, skin removed

- 2 medium heads of butter lettuce, broken into bite-sized bits, such as Boston or Bibb (approximately 1 pound),

- 2 medium tomatoes, cut into pieces of 1 inch

- 1 English medium cucumber, quartered lengthwise, then cut into 1/2 "pieces

- 1/2 cup Kalamata olives pitted, halved lengthwise

- Feta cheese, 4 ounces, crumbled (about 1 cup)

Directions

1. Arrange a middle-of-the-oven rack and heat to 425 ° F.

2. Marinate the salmon as the oven heats, and soak the onions (instructions below).

3. In a wide cup, whisk together the olive oil, vinegar, lemon juice, garlic, oregano, salt, and pepper.

4. Move 3 tablespoons of the vinaigrette to a wide enough baking dish to contain all the bits of salmon in a single layer.

5. Add the salmon and gently turn it over a few times to coat it evenly in the vinaigrette. Cover and hold refrigerated.

6. Put the onion and water in a small bowl and set aside to make the onion less potent for 10 minutes.

7. Drain the liquid and dispose of it.

8. Uncover the salmon and roast for 8 to 12 minutes until it is cooked through and flakes easily.

9. In the centre of the thickest fillet, an instant-read thermometer can record 120 ° F to 130 ° F for medium-rare, or 135 ° F to 145 ° F if you prefer it to be more well-done.

10. The total cooking time depends on the thickness of the salmon, based on the fillet's thickest section.

11. Compose a salad in the meantime.

12. In a vinaigrette dish, add the lettuce, tomato, cucumber, olives, and drained red onion and toss to coat evenly.

13. Split between four dishes or shallow bowls. Place 1 fillet on the top of each salad when the salmon is ready. Sprinkle with the feta and quickly serve.

8. Carrot, Courgette and Halloumi Hamburgers Recipe

Ingredients

- 1 big carrot, grated
- 1 large courgette, grated
- 225g halloumi, grated
- 2 spring onions, finely chopped
- 90g Bread Crumbs
- 1 tablespoon ground cumin
- 1 tablespoon ground coriander
- 1/2 teaspoon salt
- 2 tbsp. flour
- 4 brioche buns, halved
- 50g baby spinach leaves
- 1 big tomato, sliced
- 1 small red onion, chopped
- 1/2 pineapple, peeled into ribbons
- tzatziki, to function

Directions

1. Place the courgette into a clean tea towel and squeeze to eradicate any liquid.
2. Hint into a big bowl and then add the carrot, halloumi, onion, bread crumbs, cumin, coriander, eggs, salt, and flour. Stir well to mix.
3. Put simply over half the mix in a food processor and pulse until the mixture starts to stay.
4. Reunite back this into the booked mix and mix well.
5. Divide the mix into 4 and then form into patties.

6. Heat a grill or griddle pan on moderate heat.

7. Cook the hamburgers for 45 mins each side until golden and cooked through.

8. Insert the hamburger buns into the grill till lightly toasted.

9. To assemble the burgers, put lettuce leaves on the base of each bun.

10. Top with all the hamburger, a piece of tomato, pineapple ribbon along with a spoonful of tzatziki.

9. Black Bean and Sweet Potato Tacos

Ingredients

- 1 pound (about 2 medium) sweet potatoes, peeled and chopped into 1/2-inch chunks
- 2 Spoonfuls of olive oil, divided
- 1 teaspoon of kosher salt, split
- 1/4 teaspoon of black pepper, freshly ground
- 1/2 big, yellow or white onion, finely chopped
- 2 Tablespoons of chili powder
- 1/2 teaspoon cumin ground
- 1 (15-ounce) can be drained and rinsed with black beans,
- 1/4 cup water
- 1/4 cup of fresh cilantro that has been chopped
- 12 Maize Tortillas
- Guacamole-Guacamole
- Crumbled cheese with Cotija or feta (optional)
- Wedges of lime

Directions

1. Arrange a middle-of-the-oven rack and heat to 425 ° F. On a working surface, position a large sheet of aluminium foil.
2. Place on top of the tortillas and cover them tightly in the foil; set aside.
3. Place them on a rimmed baking sheet with the sweet potatoes.
4. Sprinkle with 1 tablespoon of oil and apply 1/2 teaspoon salt and 1/4 teaspoon of black pepper. Toss into a single layer to blend and distribute.
5. 20 minutes to roast. With a flat spatula, turn the potatoes over and step aside a bit to leave one corner of the baking sheet clean.

6. Place the tortillas foil pack in the empty space and continue roasting until the sweet potatoes are browned and tender and the tortillas soft, about 10 minutes longer. Cook the beans meanwhile.

7. Heat up the remaining 1 tablespoon of oil over medium-high heat in a large skillet until it shines.

8. Add the onion and cook for about 3 minutes, stirring occasionally, until tender and translucent. Stir in the chili powder, cumin, and 1/2 teaspoon of salt remaining.

9. Add the water and beans.

10. To maintain a simmer, cover the pan and reduce the heat.

11. Cook for 5 minutes, then uncover and use a fork back to partially mash the beans, leaving about half as much as possible.

12. If the pan contains any residual water, boil the uncovered mixture until it has evaporated, about 30 more seconds.

13. Attach the black beans with the roasted sweet potatoes and cilantro, and toss gently to blend.

14. Fill the tortillas with the mixture of black bean, and top with guacamole and cheese, if used. Serve with wedges of lime.

10. Vegetable Stir-Fry

Ingredients

Sauce

- 1/3 of a cup of water

- Tamari or soy sauce for 2 teaspoons

- Two teaspoons of honey or sweetened brown sugar

- 1 teaspoon of minced fresh, peeled ginger

- White or red miso paste 1 teaspoon

- 1 Cornstarch teaspoon

- 1/4 teaspoon flakes of red pepper (optional)

Stir-Fry

- 3 Spoonfuls of canola or vegetable oil, divided

- Cut into small florets, 1 1/2 pounds of broccoli (about 2 medium heads),

- Seasonal salt

- New mushrooms combined with 8 ounces, stems cut and thinly sliced

- 2 medium, cored, seeded bell peppers and cut into 1/2-inch-wide strips

- Snow Peas 8 ounces

- Garlic with 3 cloves, minced

- 1 tablespoon minced fresh peeled ginger

- Cooked rice or pasta, to serve

- 1/4 cup roasted peanuts, finely chopped

Directions

1. Whisk together all the ingredients in a small bowl, make sure the cornstarch is dissolved; set aside.

2. Make the stir-fry: over medium-high heat, heat a flat-bottomed wok, or large frying pan until a drop of water instantly vaporizes upon contact.

3. Drizzle around the pan with 1 tablespoon of oil, add the broccoli, and season with salt.

4. Stir-fry with a metal spatula until it starts to soften and brown around the edges, for 1 to 2 minutes. Move it to a wide tray.

5. In the pan, stir 1/2 tablespoon of oil, add the mushrooms, and season with salt. Stir-fry for 1 to 2 minutes, until brown and softened. Move the broccoli to the plate.

6. Add the peppers, snow peas, garlic, and ginger and season with salt.

7. Drizzle the remaining 1 1/2 tablespoons of oil in the pan. Stir-fry for about 1 minute until the garlic and ginger are fragrant and the vegetables are softened.

8. Back to the plate, add the reserved broccoli and mushrooms and any accumulated juices and swirl to blend.

9. Stir the sauce one more time, pour it into the pan, and cook for 1 to 2 minutes, stirring continuously, until the sauce thickens and coats the vegetables.

10. Serve over rice or noodles and put the peanuts on top.

11. Chicken Liver Along with tomato Ragu Recipe

Ingredients

- 2 tablespoon olive oil
- 1 onion, finely chopped
- 2 carrots, scrubbed and simmer
- 4 garlic cloves, finely chopped
- 1/4 x 30g pack fresh ginger, stalks finely chopped, leaves ripped
- 380g package poultry livers, finely chopped, and almost any sinew removed and lost
- 400g tinned Grower's Harvest chopped berries
- 1 chicken stock cube, created around 300ml
- 1/2 tsp caster sugar
- 300g penne
- 1/4 Suntrail Farms lemon, juiced

Directions

1. Heat 1 tablespoon oil in a large skillet, over a low-medium heating system.
2. Fry the onion and carrots for 10 mins, stirring periodically.
3. Stir in the ginger and garlic pops and cook 2 mins more.
4. Transfer into a bowl set aside.
5. Twist the pan into high heat and then add the oil.
6. Bring the chicken livers and simmer for 5 mins until browned.

7. Pour the onion mix into the pan and then stir in the tomatoes, sugar, and stock.

8. Season, bring to the boil, and then simmer for 20 mins until reduced and thickened, and also the liver is cooked through.

9. Meanwhile, cook pasta to package Direction.

10. Taste the ragu and put in a second pinch of sugar more seasoning, if needed.

11. Put in a squeeze of lemon juice to taste and stir in two of the ripped basil leaves.

12. Divide the pasta between four bowls, then spoon across the ragu and top with the rest of the basil.

12. Chickpea Harissa Frittata

Ingredients

- 1 Tablespoon of oil

- 1 can of Chickpeas drained,

- 1/2 cup of tomatoes dried by the sun + 1/2 teaspoon of reserved oil

- 2 Cups (fresh or frozen spinach)

- 1/2 teaspoon seasoning za'atar

- 10 whisked eggs

- One and a half cup feta cheese

- 1-2 spoonfuls of harissa sauce

- Pinch of salt and pepper

Directions

1. Preheat the oven to 350 ° F.

2. Heat a skillet of cast iron over medium heat.

3. Add olive oil and chickpeas, cook lightly, and slowly until chickpeas release liquid and start drying and browning.

4. Then add some of the reserved oil, spinach, and za'atar seasoning to the sun-dried tomatoes and cook until the spinach is wilted, 2-3 minutes.

5. Spread the vegetable mixture uniformly in the cast iron skillet when the spinach has wilted and then add the whisked eggs, rotating the pan to ensure that the vegetables are sufficiently coated with eggs.

6. Cook until the eggs start to cook about halfway through, over medium heat.

7. With spatula on the pan, do not move eggs and vegetables around, let the eggs cook without moving so the frittata sets.

8. Attach the feta cheese and spoon the harissa sauce over the top of the frittata, and sprinkle with salt and pepper, when eggs are cooked halfway through.

9. Take the cast iron skillet off the stovetop and put it in the oven on the middle rack.

10. Bake for about five minutes until the top of the frittata is cooked.

11. Remove from the oven, and slightly cool.

12. Cut into pie slices or squares to serve and remove with a spatula from the pan.

13. Minted Lamb with a Couscous Salad Recipe

Ingredients

- 75g Cous-cous

- 1/2 chicken stock block, composed of 125ml

- 30g pack refreshing flat-leaf parsley, sliced

- 3 mint sprigs, leaves picked and sliced

- 1 tablespoon olive oil

- 200g pack suspended BBQ minted lamb leg beans, De-frosted

- 200g lettuce berries, sliced

- 1/4 tsp., sliced

- 1 spring onion, sliced

- Pinch of ground cumin

- 1/2 lemon, zested and juiced

- 50g reduced-fat salad cheese

Directions

1. Place the couscous into a heatproof bowl and then pour on the inventory.

2. Cover and set aside for 10 mins, then fluff with a fork and stir in the herbs.

3. Meanwhile, rub a little oil within the lamb steaks and season.

4. Cook to package direction, then slit.

5. Mix the tomatoes, cucumber, and spring onion into the couscous with the oil, the cumin, and lemon juice, and zest. Crumble on the salad and serve with the bunny.

14. Jack Fruit Tortilla Bowls

Ingredients

- Two Sweet Corn cobettes

- 1 red chili, finely chopped

- 2 teaspoon olive oil

- 1 lime, juiced

- 15g fresh coriander, chopped, plus extra to garnish

- 150g package stained Jack Fruit in Texmex sauce

- 210g tin kidney beans, drained

- 125g roasted red peppers (in the jar), drained and chopped

- two whitened tortilla packs

- 1/2 round lettuce, ripped

Directions

1. Heat a griddle Pan at a high temperature (or light a barbecue).

2. Griddle that the cobettes to get 10 12 Mins, turning until cooked and charred throughout.

3. Remove from the pan and also stand upright onto a plank.

4. Use a sharp knife to carefully reduce the Span of this corn, staying near to the heart, to clear away the kernels.

5. Mix the kernels with the eucalyptus oil, half of the carrot juice along half of the coriander.

6. Heating the Jack fruit and sauce in a saucepan with the legumes, peppers, staying lime Coriander, and juice on medium-low heating for 3-4 mins until heated through; now.

15. Slow Cooker Easy Lentil Soup

Ingredients

- 4 cups (1 quart) of low-sodium broth for vegetables

- 1 (14-ounce) May diced tomatoes (drain not)

- 1 Little yellow onion, diced

- 1 carrot big, diced

- 1 stalk of medium celery, diced

- 1 cup lentils, green

- 1 tablespoon olive oil, plus a serving of more

- 2 Garlic cloves, minced

- 1 tsp. Kosher salt löffel

- 1 teaspoon of paste of tomato

- 1 Bay leaf

- 1/2 teaspoon cumin

- 1/2 teaspoon coriander

- 1/4 teaspoon of paprika smoked

- 2 teaspoons of Vinegar Red Wine

- Serving options: plain yogurt, olive oil, fresh chopped parsley, or cilantro leaves

Directions

1. In a 3 1/2- to a 4-quart slow cooker, put all the ingredients except the vinegar and mix to combine.

2. On the LOW environment, cover and cook until the lentils are tender around 8 hours.

3. Stir in the red wine vinegar and remove the bay leaf.

4. Add a dollop of yogurt, a drizzle of olive oil, and chopped fresh parsley or cilantro to the bowl and top if desired.

16. Curried Cauliflower Quinoa Salad

Ingredients

- 1/2 cup Yogurt

- 1 cup of cucumber in English or Persian

- Olive oil for 2 tbsp

- Tahini 1/3 cup

- 1/3 of a glass of lemon juice

- 1 Clove of Garlic, minced

- 1/2 tsp Salt

- 1 Tiny cauliflower head

- 2 tbsp Powdered curry powder

- 1/3 cup Olive oil

- Salt of 2 tsp

- 1/4 cup packed fresh cilantro leaves

- Two cups of cooked quinoa

- 2 cups of red, shredded cabbage

- 4 cup loosely packed arugula

- 2 Persian cucumbers, cut thinly

- 1 cup Golden raisins

Directions

1. Preheat the oven to 425 degrees.

2. In a wide bowl toss cauliflower with olive oil, curry powder, and salt.

3. Place in a single layer on a baking sheet and bake on the middle rack for 40 minutes.

4. Prepare the salad dressing while the cauliflower is cooking by mixing all the ingredients in a blender and blending until smooth.

5. Toss the cooked quinoa, red cabbage, and arugula together in a wide bowl and divide them into 4 cups.

6. Put fresh cilantro, cucumbers, golden raisins, and roasted cauliflower on top of each dish. Drizzle with yogurt tahini dressing and enjoy!

7. Prepare the salad dressing while the cauliflower is cooking by mixing all the ingredients in a blender and blending until smooth.

8. Toss the cooked quinoa, red cabbage, and arugula together in a wide bowl and divide them into 4 cups.

9. Put fresh cilantro, cucumbers, golden raisins, and roasted cauliflower on top of each dish. Drizzle with yogurt tahini dressing and enjoy!

17. Smoked Salmon Sushi Bowls

Ingredients

- 2 cups of rice * cooked

- Dressing with ginger sesame

- Ginger 2 inches, grated

- 1 clove Garlic, pressed

- 1 spoonful plus 1 teaspoon of sesame oil

- 1 tablespoon of soy sauce (make sure, if possible, it's gluten-free soy sauce. Or use amino tamari or coconut)

- Around 1 to 2 teaspoons of honey

- 3 tablespoon rice vinegar

- Optional: Pinch Flakes of Red Pepper

- Spicy mayo

- Mayonnaise 2 teaspoons

- Sriracha 3 to 4 teaspoons

- 1/2 teaspoon soy sauce (gluten-free, if appropriate. Or use tamari or coconut aminos)

Bowls

- Smoked salmon 12 ounces

- 1 to 2 mature, seeded, peeled, and sliced avocados

- 1 seedless cucumber, shaved into strips with a veggie peeler or julienned cucumber,

- 1 to 2 carrots, shaved with a veggie peeler or julienned nori seaweed, cut into strips using kitchen shears (I use toasted nori snacks)

Toppings

- Sliced green onion

- pickled ginger (found in the Asian section of a grocery store)

- Paste of wasabi

- sesame seeds

Directions

1. For the rice: If you haven't already made the rice do this now and allow it to cool. I used fast-cooking brown rice (10 minutes) for convenience and nutrition but you can use any kind of rice you want. Bear in mind that regular rice cooking normally takes between 30 and 45 minutes to prepare accordingly.

2. Make ginger sesame dressing: In a small mixing bowl, add all the ingredients and whisk until well mixed. Taste as needed and change the flavors. Set aside the sauce.

3. Make the spicy mayo: Add the mayonnaise, Sriracha, and soy sauce into a small mixing bowl and whisk until well mixed. Add more mayo for less spice and more Sriracha for more spice, to taste and change flavors as needed. Set spicy mayo aside.

4. Prepare veggies and salmon: Prepare all the veggies as directed above along with peeling the layers of the salmon apart. I used a Y-shaped veggie peeler to produce thin strips to cut the veggies. With a sharp knife or even a mandolin, you could also julienne the veggies.

5. Arrange the veggies Optional party step: I figured it would be fun to arrange the veggies, smoked salmon, and other toppings on a platter or cheese board if you serve these sushi bowls to guests and encourage guests to create their own sushi bowls. You might really have fun with this and even add more vegetables or other sushi ingredients. This move will be

optional. You can skip that step and just build each bowl in a less fancy way if you serve these bowls as a casual dinner for the family.

6. Top it with some smoked salmon, sliced avocado, carrots, cucumber, nori strips, and a sprinkle of green onions, plus any other toppings you want to add. Create the bowls: add some rice to a bowl. Spoon over some of the ginger sesame sauce and drizzle over some of the spicy mayo. Enjoy yourself instantly.

7. Leftovers: Put any leftovers in separate airtight containers. Right before you eat them, I find it easiest to cook the vegetables, so I recommend just chopping as many vegetables for as many servings as you need for that meal. In the refrigerator, the rice and sauces are kept well for up to 1 week.

18. Thai Coconut Curry Soup with Shrimp

Ingredients

- 2 teaspoons vegetable oil

- 3 cloves of garlic, minced

- 1 tablespoon ginger, minced

- 3 tablespoons of red Thai Curry Paste

- Shrimp 1/2 lb, peeled and deveined

- 3 cups of broth with chicken (or vegetable broth)

- 1 of a cup of water

- 2 tablespoons sauce for fish

- 2/3 cup of milk with coconut

- 6 oz. Noodles

- 1 lime

Directions

1. Add the oil, garlic, ginger, and Thai red curry paste to a large pot over medium-high heat. Stir for a few minutes before fragrant.

2. Add chicken broth, water, coconut milk, and fish sauce. Taste the broth after boiling and adjust the seasoning accordingly.

3. Stir in the shrimp and cook until they're absolutely pink.

4. Add the noodles to the pot and cook until the noodles are fully cooked.

5. Until serving, squeeze lime juice into the broth.

19. Cajun Steak and Veg Rice Jar

Ingredients

- 1 tablespoon vegetable oil
- 1 celery stick, finely chopped
- 3 large carrots, sliced into rounds
- 250g frozen chopped mixed peppers
- 4 spring onions, chopped, green and white parts split
- 500g 5 percent beef mince
- 2 teaspoon seasoning
- 1 teaspoon tomato purée
- 2 x 250g packs ready-cooked long-grain rice

Directions

1. Heat the oil in a large, shallow skillet over moderate heat.
2. Add the carrots, celery, peppers, and snowy areas of the nuts.
3. Cook for 10 mins before the veg is beginning to soften.
4. Insert the mince, season liberally, and cook for 10 mins before mince is browned and start to really go crispy.
5. Insert the Cajun seasoning and tomato purée; stir fry to coat the mince.
6. Hint inside the rice combined with 4 tablespoons of plain water.
7. Stir to completely unite heat and heat until the rice is hot. Scatter on the rest of the spring onion before serving.

20. Pesto Salmon Pasta Noodles

Ingredients

- 350g penne

- 2 x 212g tins cherry salmon, drained

- 1 lemon, zested and juiced

- 190g jar green pesto

- 250g package cherry tomatoes halved

- 100g bunch spring onions, finely chopped

- 125g package reduced-fat mozzarella

Directions

1. Pre heats the oven to Windows 7, 220°C, buff 200°C. Boil the pasta for 5 mins. Drain, reserving 100ml drinking water.

2. Meanwhile, at a 2ltr ovenproof dish, then mix the salmon, lemon zest, and juice, then pesto (booking 2 tablespoons)berries and half of the spring onions; season.

3. Mix the pasta and reserved cooking water to the dish. Mix the allowed pesto using 1 tablespoon water and then drizzle on the pasta.

4. Gently within the mozzarella, top with the rest of the spring onions, and bake for 25 mins until golden.

21. Masala Chickpea Buddha Bowl

Ingredients

Masala Chickpeas

- 2 tablespoons of coconut (or olive oil) oil

- 2 onions, sliced

- 1 clove of garlic, minced

- 1 medium-sized carrot, cut into 2-inch pieces

- 1 red bell pepper, chopped

- 1 teaspoon of grated ginger

- 1 teaspoon salt

- 1 tsp of each: garam masala, turmeric, cumin, coriander, paprika

- 2 and 1/2 cup water

- 1 15-oz can cooked chickpeas, drained and rinsed

Quinoa

- 1/2 cup (I used black quinoa) quinoa

- 1 and 1/4 cup water

- Soy sauce for 1 tbsp

Spinach

- 3 cups (rinsed) chopped spinach

- 1 garlic clove

- salt, pepper

Optional (Toppings)

- 1 cup red cabbage, finely shredded

- 1/4 cup roasted cashews that are slightly crushed

- If you like it, new parsley, or cilantro,

- Red pepper crushed

Directions

1. Heat the coconut oil in a large skillet over medium heat.

2. Once the oil is hot, add the onions, garlic, and grated ginger and cook on medium heat until the onions are soft and translucent around 5-7 minutes.

3. Add the carrot and red bell pepper, continue to cook for another 2 minutes. Add spices and salt and cover with the water.

4. Bring to a boil, cover, and reduce heat. Let simmer for around 35 minutes, or until vegetables are tender. In the meantime, you should start the quinoa.

5. Remove from the heat and process until silky smooth in a blender. Pour the sauce back into the skillet and stir in the chickpeas. Cover to keep warm.

6. Combine the quinoa with the water and soy sauce in a medium saucepan. Bring to a boil, reduce heat and simmer until the quinoa is cooked for about 25 minutes or until almost no liquid remains.

7. Heat some olive oil in a pan, add the garlic and sauté for 2-3 minutes. Add spinach and cook for 5-7 minutes until the spinach is wilted. Season with salt and pepper.

8. Divide the quinoa into three serving bowls and cover it with spinach and masala chickpeas. Top with crushed cashews, red cabbage, and fresh herbs.

22. Chicken Noodle Stir-fry

Ingredients

- 1 tablespoon sunflower oil

- 750g package chicken thighs, boned, any surplus skin trimmed

- 250g frozen chopped mixed peppers

- Inch courgette, peeled into ribbons, seeded centre chopped

- 1 chicken stock cube

- 250g pack moderate egg yolks

- 4 garlic cloves, finely chopped

- 1/2 tsp crushed chilies, and additional to serve (optional)

- 4 tablespoons reduced-salt soy sauce

- 2 tsp caster sugar

- 1 lime, zested, 1/2 juiced, 1/2 slice into wedges to function

Directions

1. Heat the oil in a skillet on a medium-low warmth.

2. Fry the chicken skin-side down to 10 mins or until your skin is emptied.

3. Flip and simmer for 10 mins, or until cooked. Transfer to a plate cover loosely with foil.

4. Reheat the wok over a high temperature, add the peppers and sliced courgette; simmer for 5 mins.

5. Meanwhile, bring a bowl of water to the boil, then crumble in the stock block, adding the noodles.

6. Simmer for 45 mins until cooked, then drain well.

7. Insert the garlic and crushed chilies into the wok; simmer for two mins. In a bowl, mix the soy sugar and the lime juice and zest.

8. Enhance the wok, bubble 2 mins; you can add the courgette noodles and ribbons.

9. Toss with tongs to coat in the sauce.

10. Cut the chicken into pieces.

11. Divide the noodles between 4 bowls and top with the chicken.

12. Serve with the lime wedges along with extra crushed chilies, in case you prefer.

23. Chili-Lime Tilapia

Ingredients

- 3 fillets of tilapia (or any white fish, if possible, caught wild)

- 1 big sweet potato, sliced into fries (or 2 medium ones)

- The head of 1 broccoli, cut into florets

- 1/2 cup of freshly squeezed lime juice (or 2-lime juice)

- 1/4 of a cup of chopped fresh cilantro

- 2 tablespoons olive oil + 2 for veggies

- 2 spoonfuls of water

- 1 tbsp. of honey

- 1 tablespoon of minced garlic (or 4 garlic cloves crushed)

- 1 teaspoon of red flakes of chili, or to taste,

- Chili powder for 1/2 teaspoon

- 1/8 teaspoon cumin ground

- Salt and fresh cracked pepper

- For garnish, 2 tablespoons of chopped cilantro leaves

- 1 small pepper bird-eye, sliced for garnish, optional

Directions

1. Preheat your oven to 210 ° C (425 ° F). Oil a baking sheet thinly or brush with non-stick spray.

2. In a small bowl, whisk together 2 tablespoons of olive oil, water, garlic, lime juice, honey, chili flakes, cumin, chili powder, and cilantro.

3. On the prepared baking sheet, put the sweet potato fries and broccoli in a single layer.

4. Add 2 tablespoons of olive oil; season to taste with salt and pepper and blend well.

5. Create some space for the fillets of white fish and put tilapia in the spaces reserved.

6. Brush the chili-lime mixture with the fish.

7. Bake with a fork until the fish flakes easily and the broccoli starts to crisp up on the edges and soften about 20-25 minutes.

8. If desired, serve the baked tilapia garnished with cilantro, chili peppers in slices, and lime wedges.

9. Enjoy!

24. White Beans with Olive Oil Toast

Ingredients

- 2 Drained and rinsed 15-ounce cans of white beans (great northern / cannellini),

- Olive oil for 6 tablespoons

- 2 teaspoons vinegar with red wine

- 1 Juiced Lemon

- 2 teaspoons of new basil chopped

- 2 teaspoons of fresh cilantro, chopped

- 1 tablespoon of fresh parsley chopped

- Two honey teaspoons

- 2 minced garlic cloves

- 1/4 dried oregano teaspoon

- 1/4 of a teaspoon of salt

- 1/4 of the pepper teaspoon

- 1/4 teaspoon of crushed flakes of red pepper

- 2 ounces of crumbled feta cheese

- 1/4 cup of roasted red pepper chopped

- 2 tablespoons of sun-dried sliced tomatoes

Directions

1. In a wide bowl, put the beans.

2. Blend the oil, vinegar, lemon juice, spices, honey, garlic, oregano salt, pepper, and red pepper flakes in a small cup.

3. Pour the beans on.

4. Stir in the feta cheese, tomatoes, and red peppers.

5. Cover the bowl in plastic wrap and stick it for at least 30 minutes in the refrigerator.

6. That way, it will have the most flavour, but you can obviously eat it immediately!

7. To make the olive oil toasts, openly drizzle your favourite olive oil bread!

8. Over medium heat, heat a skillet and add the bread to the skillet once it is heated.

9. Toast until it is golden brown and crunchy on either side. Serve on top of the toast with the beans!

25. Millet Risotto with Spring Vegetables and Seared Scallops

Ingredients

- 10 (approx 1/2 lb) bay scallops
- 1 of a cup of millet
- 4 cups of seafood stock (or chicken)
- A cup of 1/4 of white wine
- 1 cup of peas fresh
- 1 bunch of asparagus, ends cut and cut into segments of 1
- 2 shallots, minced shallots,
- 2 Tbsp. of butter
- 2 tbs. of olive oil, split
- Pepper and salt

Directions

1. Warm stock in a small saucepan over medium heat.
2. Once warm, over low heat, keep on the stove.
3. Heat 1 tbsp. olive oil in a large saucepan or Dutch oven over medium-high heat until it shimmers. If the oil is hot, add the millet and stir in the toast for about 2 minutes.
4. Add wine, stir and make sure any brown bits are scraped from the bottom of the pot.
5. Add stock after the wine has evaporated, 1 ladle at a time, making sure to stir constantly as stock is consumed.
6. All of the stock should be added after about 30 minutes and the millet will be creamy and al-dente.

7. With salt and pepper, season generously, and keep warm.

8. Melt 2 tbsp of butter in a large skillet over medium-high heat.

9. Asparagus and shallot should be added when the butter is melted and foamed.

10. Sauté until the asparagus has browned slightly, around 3 minutes.

11. Attach the peas and proceed to cook for another 1 minute. With salt and pepper, season.

12. Apply the mixture of spring vegetables to the millet risotto and swirl to blend. Just keep wet.

13. Thoroughly dry the scallops and season with salt.

14. Return 1 tbs of olive oil in a large skillet to high-heat and warm until barely smoking.

15. To pan and cook, carefully add scallops, taking care not to overload the skillet (cook if possible in two batches).

16. Sear scallops, 2 minutes undisturbed.

17. Flip for an extra 2 minutes and sear. Remove from the skillet to a lined paper towel tray.

18. Top risotto with seared scallops for service.

Chapter 4. 3 Days Pescatarian Diet Meal Plan

Day 1

Breakfast

Avocado Baked Eggs

Ingredients

- 1 avocado

- 1/4 cup lemon juice

- 2 eggs

- Pinch of salt

- Pinch of black pepper

- A handful (chopped) of cilantro

Directions

1. Preheat your oven to 220 Celsius / 425 Fahrenheit.

2. Cut the avocado in half using a sharp knife, extracting the seed with the hands or a spoon.

3. To fit your egg in, you may want to scoop out a slightly larger hole inside each avocado half. With a teaspoon, this is reasonably easy to do.

4. Squeeze on the tops of the avocado halves over the juice from the lemon portion.

5. In the oven, this will avoid them turning orange.

6. Now smash your eggs into each of the avocado halves and add to the top of each one a pinch of salt and pepper.

7. Place them on a small baking tray or inside a muffin tin (helping them stay upright) and position them for 15 minutes in the oven.

8. Until they are ready, let them stand before serving them for 1 minute.

Lunch

Moroccan Stuffed Sweet Potato Skins

Ingredients

- 2 sweet potatoes
- 1 can of drained chickpea
- 2 cloves of finely chopped garlic
- 2 tsp. of cumin
- 1 handful of finely chopped parsley
- 1 tsp. of coriander
- 1 tsp. paprika
- 1/2 tsp. salt
- 1/2 tsp. black pepper
- 40 Feta cheese, sliced into cubes

Directions

1. Start by heating the oven to 370° Fahrenheit / 180° Celsius in advance.

2. Place the sweet potatoes on a baking tray, cut them with a knife into a few shallow slits, and place them for about 40 minutes in the oven to roast.

3. Grab a big bowl and add the chickpeas, garlic, parsley, cumin, cilantro, and paprika while the sweet potatoes are roasting.

4. Only blend them well together.

5. Remove the sweet potatoes from the oven and horizontally cut them in half. Scoop the sweet potato out, leaving the skin with around 2 cm of sweet potato attached.

6. Cut the sweet potato into pieces of bite-size and blend into the chickpeas so that the spices are hidden.

7. Take the bowl's contents and spoon back into the skins of the sweet potato.

8. Attach the feta cubes, then put them back in the oven for 15 minutes. Remove from the oven and serve until hot!

Dinner

Thai Massaman Curry

Ingredients

- Paste for Curry

- 1 (finely chopped) red chili.

- 1 chili in green (finely chopped)

- 1 teaspoon galangal

- 1 Tsp of cilantro seeds

- 1 teaspoon of fresh ginger

- 2 garlic cloves (finely chopped)

- 30 g (finely chopped) new coriander

- 1 Tsp nutmeg field

- 1 tablespoon of turmeric

- 1 tbsp cumin field

- 10ml of oil for vegetables

- Soy Sauce 10ml

- Fish sauce 10ml

Curry

- 1 broad leaf of bay

- Coconut Cream 160ml

- 400ml of milk from a coconut

- 200 g of white potatoes (peeled and sliced into bites)

- (cut into quarters) 3 shallots

- Cashew nuts for 50 g

Directions

1. Place a large wok over a heavy heat.

2. Add the turmeric, nutmeg, ground cumin, and coriander seeds once the pan has heated up (make sure you grind the seeds using a pestle and mortar into a powder).

3. Make sure when you do this, there is no moisture in the pan because you simply want to dry the powders to roast to release their flavour.

4. This should only take about 30 seconds and as soon as you pass them about, you should start smelling the scent of the spices.

5. Add vegetable oil, chili pepper, fresh cilantro, garlic, ginger, soy sauce, galangal, and fish sauce.

6. For another 30 seconds, stir the pan constantly until all the flavors are blended into a wet paste.

7. Throw in and stir in the shallots, potatoes, and cashew nuts until finely covered in the paste.

8. Apply the coconut cream, coconut milk and bay leaves and blend well with the mixture.

9. Boil the pan and then reduce the heat so it's just simmering.

10. For around 25-30 minutes, leave the curry to simmer, remove the bay leaf, and it'll be ready to eat.

Day 2

Breakfast

Spanish Egg Muffins

Ingredients

- Olive oil glug

- 1 shallot, thinly sliced

- 1 garlic cloves, thinly minced

- 1/4 red, finely chopped pepper

- 1/4 green, finely chopped pepper

- Tomatoes of 60 g

- 1/2 tsp of paprika

- 6 eggs of broad size

Directions

1. Preheat the oven to 390 Fahrenheit/ 200 Celsius.

2. At medium heat, put a small frying pan and pour the olive oil in.

3. Add in the shallot when the oil is hot, then leave to sweat for 3 minutes with the lid on.

4. Then add the garlic, peppers, tomatoes, paprika, and sweat for another 5 minutes, stirring regularly to make sure they don't stay together. Turn the heat off and allow the side of the pan to cool.

5. Beat the 6 eggs in a big jug or cup. Attach your frying pan to the contents and season with salt and pepper.

6. Spoon your muffin tray with the ingredients at night and put them in the oven for about 15 minutes, until the muffins are soft and springy, then remove them from the oven and you're finished!

Lunch

Mac N Cheese

Ingredients

- 220g pasta macaroni

- 30g of butter

- 3 cloves of garlic, minced garlic, minced garlic

- 2 tbsp. flour

- 325ml Milk

- 100g Cheddar, grated

- 1/2 tsp. Paprika

- 2/3 cauliflower head, florets in bite-size cut

- 40g Spinach

- A handful of breadcrumbs

- 30 g of Parmesan, grated

Directions

1. Preheat your oven to 180 Celsius / 360 Fahrenheit

2. Start by boiling your macaroni as instructed. It should only take 6-7 minutes, as it is a small pasta.

3. Drain and leave on the side until cooked.

4. When the heat is low, heat a large saucepan and add the butter.

5. Then put your minced garlic in and let the garlic cook for a few minutes.

6. Then apply the flour, a tablespoon at a time, and use a wooden spoon to mix with the butter.

7. First, to ensure the sauce stays smooth and lump-free, you need to add the milk slowly, whisking as you go.

8. Next, remove the heat from the saucepan and whisk in much of the cheddar slowly, leaving a small handful.

9. Then do the same with the Parmesan, leaving just enough at the end to sprinkle over your plate.

10. Now stir in your macaroni, cauliflower, spinach, and paprika, making sure your wonderful cheese sauce is all coated with it.

11. At first, the spinach will look like a lot but will wilt down really soon.

12. Now pour your mac & cheese and scatter your breadcrumbs, cheddar, and parmesan in an oven-proof bowl.

13. Finally, place your scrumptious mac & cheese in the oven and leave until the top is golden and crispy for about 30-40 minutes.

Dinner

Baked Tilapia with Parmesan Crust

Ingredients

- 2 filets of tilapia
- 100g of vegetarian parmesan, finely grated
- 40g of breadcrumbs
- 1 handful of finely chopped parsley
- 1.5 tsp. paprika
- 1 tsp. Black pepper
- 3 tablespoons olive oil
- 1 lemon, sweet with wedges

Directions

1. Start by preheating the oven to 200° Celsius / 400° Fahrenheit.

2. Mix the grated parmesan, breadcrumbs, paprika, black pepper, and parsley together in a mixing dish. On a big, flat baking tray spread the mixture and leave it on one side.

3. Mix the lemon and olive oil together in a small jug, take just under half of the olive oil mixture and fry 1 tilapia fillet on both sides, then dip it into the Parmesan mixture, covering the whole fillet.

4. With the second fillet, then repeat the procedure, leaving a little leftover oil.

5. Check for any places where the crust does not adhere and dab a little extra oil on it until both tilapia fillets have been coated, followed by a sprinkling of the Parmesan mix.

6. Place both tilapia fillets in the oven and leave for around 20 minutes to cook.

7. When the crust turns a golden brown colour and the fresh tilapia is white and flaky, you will know the tilapia we made.

Day 3

Breakfast

Huevos Rancheros (149 Calories)

Ingredients

- 1/2 red pepper, sliced into strips
- 1/2 orange pepper, sliced into strips
- 4 quartered grape tomatoes.
- 1 garlic clove, finely chopped
- 1 onion, diced
- 1 tbsp. Smoked paprika
- 4 Eggs in the Free Range
- 50g Pinto Beans
- 50g Kidney beans
- 1 tin of sliced tomatoes
- 1 tbsp. Rapeseed oil

Directions

1. Over high heat, put a deep frying pan and pour the rapeseed oil in.
2. You may use vegetable oil if you don't have rapeseed oil, so it's only the rapeseed oil that is a little better.
3. Add the onion, tomatoes, and garlic to the saucepan and fry for 5 minutes, stirring frequently.
4. Add the tomatoes, pinto beans, butter beans, and kidney beans, until the onion has softened.

5. To take the tartness out of them, pour over the tin of tomatoes and add a pinch of sugar.

6. Finally, mix the smoked paprika and add salt and pepper to the seasoning.

7. Switch the heater down to medium heat and cook for 15 minutes, stirring periodically.

8. Create four small wells in the mixture using the back of a large serving spoon and crack an egg into each.

9. Right now, turn the heat down and cook for an additional 3-4 minutes or until the egg whites turn white.

10. Take the pan away from the heat after this has happened and leave it to stand for a few minutes.

11. With some flatbread, serve the meal and enjoy it as an energizing breakfast or brunch meal.

Lunch

Mackerel & Green Bean Salad

Ingredients

- 4 big eggs
- 90 g Sugar Snap Peas
- 100 g Green beans
- 50 g peas from the greenhouse
- 1 avocado, peeled and cube-cut
- 60 g mixed salad leaves from spring
- 50 g Mackrel
- 1/4 lemon juice
- 1 tablespoon black pepper

Directions

1. Start putting a saucepan of boiling water over medium heat.
2. Add the eggs to the mixture and leave for 3 minutes.
3. Then add the green beans and the sugar snap peas to the water and cook for another 3 minutes.
4. Remove the eggs and run them under cold water briefly.
5. Drain the snap peas with green beans and sugar.
6. Put the salad leaves, green beans, sugar snap peas, garden peas, avocado mackerel, and lemon juice in a large salad bowl.
7. Give a decent mix to the salad, then de-shell the eggs and quarter them over the salad so that the yolk flows over the salad, add the white egg to the salad, and you're ready to serve!

Dinner

Teriyaki Stir-fry

Ingredients

- 4 big eggs
- 90g sugar snap peas
- 100g green beans
- 50g peas from the greenhouse
- 1 avocado, peeled and cube-cut
- 60g mixed salad leaves from spring
- 50g mackerel
- 1/4 lemon juice
- 1 tbsp. black pepper

Directions

1. Start putting a saucepan of boiling water over medium heat.
2. Add the eggs to the mixture and leave for 3 minutes.
3. Then add the green beans and the sugar snap peas to the water and cook for another 3 minutes.
4. Remove the eggs and run them under cold water briefly.
5. Drain the snap peas with green beans and sugar.
6. Put the salad leaves, green beans, sugar snap peas, garden peas, avocado mackerel, and lemon juice in a large salad bowl.

7. Give a decent mix to the salad, then de-shell the eggs and quarter them over the salad so that the yolk flows over the salad, add the white egg to the salad, and you're ready to serve!

CPSIA information can be obtained
at www.ICGtesting.com
Printed in the USA
LVHW060346120221
679113LV00004B/133